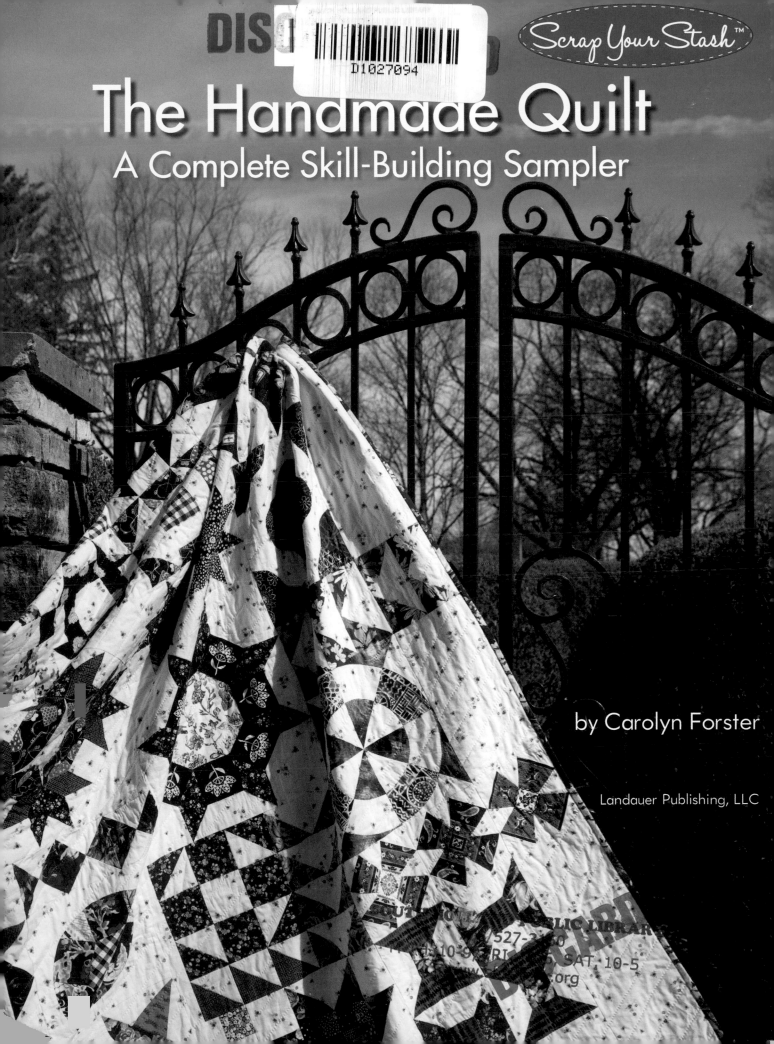

D1027094

Scrap Your Stash™

The Handmade Quilt
A Complete Skill-Building Sampler

by Carolyn Forster

Landauer Publishing, LLC

The Handmade Quilt
A Complete Skill-Building Sampler

by Carolyn Forster

Copyright © 2018 by Landauer Publishing, LLC
Projects Copyright © 2018 by Carolyn Forster
This book was designed, produced,
and published by Landauer Publishing, LLC
3100 100th Street, Urbandale, IA 50322
515/287/2144   800/557/2144   landauerpub.com

President/Publisher: Jeramy Lanigan Landauer
Editor/Art Director: Laurel Albright
Editor/Photographer: Sue Voegtlin

All rights reserved. No part of this book may be reproduced or
transmitted in any form by any means, electronic or mechanical,
including photocopying, recording, or by any information
storage and retrieval system without permission in writing
from the publisher with the exception that the publisher grants
permission to enlarge the template patterns in this book for
personal use only. The scanning, uploading and distribution of
this book or any part thereof, via the Internet or any other means
without permission from the publisher is illegal and punishable
by law. The publisher presents the information in this book in
good faith. No warranty is given, nor are results guaranteed.

Library of Congress: 2018938289

ISBN 13: 978-1-935726-96-8
This book printed on acid-free paper.

10-9-8-7-6-5-4-3-2-1

3 1350 00375 0801

Landauer Books are distributed
to the Trade by
Fox Chapel Publishing
1970 Broad Street
East Petersburg, PA 17520
www.foxchapelpublishing.com
1-800-457-9112

For consumer orders:
Landauer Publishing, LLC
3100 100th Street
Urbandale, Iowa 50322
www.landauerpub.com
1-800-557-2144

About the Author

Carolyn Forster, quilt maker, teacher and author, has been sewing and creating for as long as she can remember. Since stitching her first quilt from 1" fabric squares at the age of 17, she has been hooked on patchwork and quilting.

Carolyn's love of quilting sends her to many places teaching, lecturing and sharing her favorite quilting techniques. She has authored a number of patchwork and quilting books in the UK and America. Carolyn lives in Royal Tunbridge Wells, in the south east of England, with her husband and son, and a lot of fabric.

In memory of Mary O'Higgins

To find out more about hand stitching, or to contact Carolyn about classes, go to:
www.carolynforster.co.uk
E-mail: carolynforster@hotmail.co.uk

Introduction

When I meet with a new group of students, I'm frequently asked these questions:

"I don't have a machine" or "I don't want to lug my sewing machine to class. Is it okay if I sew by hand?"

"If I stitch by hand will my quilt be strong enough?"

"Won't it be slower to stitch by hand?"

The answers are simple:

Yes, it's okay to sew by hand. Before sewing machines were invented, quilts were always hand sewn.

Yes, your quilt will be "strong enough". Hand stitched quilts have survived over a hundred years and repairs are just as easy as if you machine stitch.

Time spent hand stitching or machine sewing is relative to when, where, and how you choose to spend your allotted time for sewing.

Let me explain from the beginning...

I have sewn quilts for many years. When I first started, I didn't have a sewing machine so I stitched by hand. That's how I learned. I enjoyed the pace when hand stitching, and the fact I could stitch almost anywhere in peace and quiet.

When I could afford a sewing machine to make patchwork quilts, it was quite a contrast to stitching by hand. But when I started sewing with a machine, I enjoyed a change of pace—speed! Things came together quickly and I liked the different methods and approaches a sewing machine had to offer. I realized some patchwork blocks went together better by machine, and others were actually easier by hand.

Now I had two sets of skills—one for hand piecing and one for machine piecing. I could determine which one suited the time I allotted for sewing. While it was faster, sewing with a machine required me to sit at one. Sewing by hand could be done almost anywhere. It was portable; I could sew while riding in the car, while watching TV or quietly sitting outside in a calm and peaceful environment. Having the choice between machine and hand stitching was liberating!

I teach both machine and hand pieced patchwork. One of the biggest contrasts in these classes is the pace, atmosphere, and "vibe" that begins to evolve when hand stitching. The conversations that start, the world being put right, confidences shared, seem to allow us to come out of these classes refreshed and ready for the rest of the day, something that benefits everyone.

Learning to hand piece your patchwork can open up personal time and space that is often needed with today's frenetic lifestyles. As you stitch you build up a rhythm of working and with that, it is easy to let thoughts wander and distill. It gives you a chance to get lost in your thoughts and let go of stress as you focus on the task at hand. It's a therapeutic benefit and quite often a new creativity is born.

By taking the time to sew by hand you are renewing your patience and showing yourself that, actually, it doesn't take as long as you thought it would. That, in itself, is a refreshing thought. The process turns out to be as rewarding as the end product.

A machine is not a necessity to make a quilt. With a few basic techniques, a needle and thread, and your own two hands, you can make a quilt. I encourage you to give hand stitching a try. In this fast-paced world it's okay to slow down, decompress, and create a beautiful quilt totally by hand.

Carolyn

Contents

SOUTH HOLLAND PUBLIC LIBRARY
708/527-3150
M-TH. 10-9, FRI. 10-6, SAT. 10-5
www.shlibrary.org

Getting Started

Equipment for Hand Piecing Patchwork

Hand piecing patchwork requires very little basic equipment to get started. Pins, needles, thread, scissors, maybe a thimble or two, is basically all you need once the pieces have been cut.

Not everyone will stitch the same or use the same equipment. If you are happy with the results using the things you have, that's great! But it's always worth trying something new or different rather than always using what you have. Remember,

"If you do what you always do, you will get what you always get".

Scissors

Choose a pair of scissors that you are happy to hold! I like scissors with a serrated edge because they seem to grip the fabric as they cut. Regardless of what you choose, make sure the blades are sharp.

Dedicate a pair of scissors that you will use only to cut batting and template plastic or card stock. It will ensure that your fabric scissors stay sharp.

Use a small pair of scissors or thread snips for the sole purpose of cutting thread. They are easier to handle and very portable. Many small scissors have a sheath to protect the blades while adding a safety factor when reaching for them in your sewing bag.

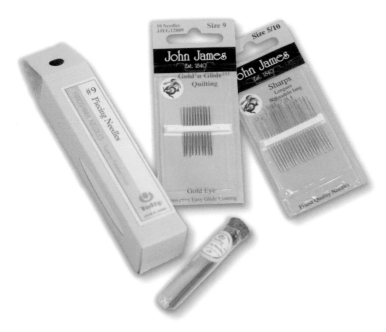

Needles

Sew with a needle that you are comfortable with, one that will hold the thread without coming out of the eye, and will pull through the fabric easily with no tugging needed. A good, all-purpose needle for most people is Sharps. They are medium length with a round eye and a sharp point.

I like to use size 10 quilting needles or size 9 piecing needles. You can buy piecing needles for patchwork that are longer but they need a different sewing action because of their length. Sharps are a good general needle that work well for most people.

Two of my favorite needle makers are John James and Tulip. They are easy to find and offer a variety of specialty needles including ones with round or long eyes for easy threading.

Pins

It is worth investing in quality pins that are sharp because it will help with accuracy when you are pinning pieces together. I like to use either long and fine pins with glass heads, or short and neat pins like applique pins. Most often, I use Clover short applique pins or Clover Patchwork pins.

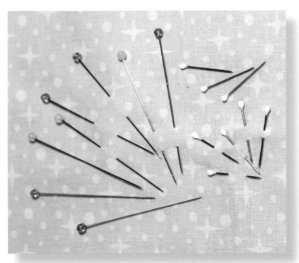

Thread

Believe it or not, an uninspiring thread set of basic "shadow" colors is all you need for most hand stitching. Colors like the ones shown here, creams, grays, tans, black, and a muddy gray green, will merge with most fabrics.

Since I am constantly sewing, I buy thread in the most economical way I can. I buy large spools of limited colors, which makes the most sense for my needs. If I need my work to be portable, I'll buy smaller spools or wind thread around one of my extra machine bobbins or and empty spool.

Aurifil 28 weight (small spools, upper left) is my favorite thread for hand sewing. It's a bit thicker than 40 or 50 weight. Try the 40 or 50 weight if you prefer something closer to the thread you use for machine stitching. Different brands of thread will handle differently so you may need to experiment until you find your favorite.

Needle Threaders

If I'm threading a needle by hand, I find it easier to put the needle over the thread rather than trying to push the thread through the eye (see page 19). But there are many devices to make needle threading a breeze. From the simple ones that sometimes are included with a pack of needles to the more sophisticated, they are time saving tools to get you started stitching.

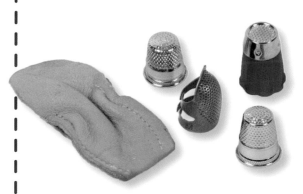

Thimbles

Thimbles are often the most controversial subject of sewing. I didn't always use a thimble; I braved sore fingers and chipped nails until I had had enough! I went through finger protectors, tape, wraps, and leather sheaths. By experimenting, it got me used to stitching with something on the end of my fingers.

They all worked but I eventually realized I could sew with a ridged, flat top thimble on my index finger underneath my work and one a dimpled metal thimble on my middle finger on top of my work. This works best for me but once again, trial and error may be the best path when determining your favorite thimble and how to use it.

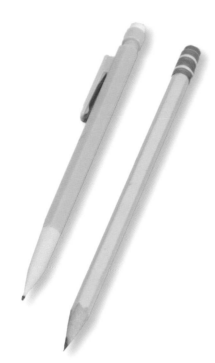

Fabric Markers

Mechanical fabric pencils with a fine tip will always give a clear, fine line. And mechanical pencils don't need sharpening! They will often come in colors which makes it easier to see on fabric. A standard pencil with hard lead will always work, too.

Fabric Choice and Quantities

For the quilt in this book, I chose to use navy and creams for the blocks and binding. Your color choice can be whatever you want but take the time to decide what kind of fabric will work well for hand stitching.

I find it easier to stitch with 100 percent cotton fabrics that are dress or craft weight. I like to prewash all of my fabric to minimize color bleed and shrinkage. While it isn't necessary only you can decide what is best for you and your quilt.

To add some body to lighter weight fabrics, try spritzing with a spray starch product. Besides adding body, it will stabilize the fabric when you are tracing on it but still stay easy to stitch.

I used a scrappy combination of fabrics for the quilt in the book. I suggest you start off with four or five fat quarters that you like together. I would allow one fat quarter (18" x 22") for each block. Some may use all of it and some less. As you make your way through the blocks you can use up the scraps or introduce more fabrics as you work.

See page 97 for complete fabric requirements for the quilt.

Templates

Preparing and Cutting Templates

There are several ways to cut fabric when you start piecing. You can use templates, a rotary cutter, or die cut tools that are on the market today. Each method will have its own advantages and it's worth considering each to see what works best for you.

Templates can be used to cut out fabric. Some templates used to trace on fabric don't include a seam allowance. Others will include it. Either way, you will need to keep in mind some basic tips when making and using templates.

Card Stock

The quickest and easiest way for many of us is to photocopy the shapes and glue them to firm card stock. This technique works well if you only plan on using the template for a couple of blocks. Each time you draw around the card, the edges will soften and the shape will change a little with multiple use. I use card stock for single use templates when I want to get a quick idea of how a block will turn out.

1 Photocopy the templates onto copy paper. Check the copy against the templates in the book to make sure they are accurate. Rough cut around the template, leaving 1/2" or so around the outside.

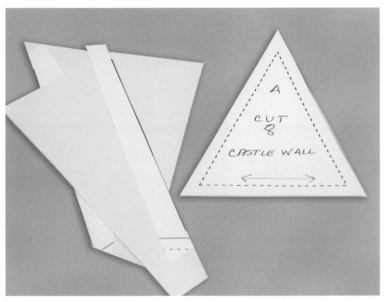

2 Glue the wrong side of the paper template onto card stock and cut out the shapes directly on the solid lines. After cutting, label your templates with a name, grain line, and any other information important to that piece.

Template Plastic

When you want to use a template for more than a few cuts, template plastic is a more durable option. I suggest using a fine line permanent marker to keep your template the correct size when cutting it out. The templates in this book include the seam allowances. But it's a good idea to know how to add it when it isn't included on a template.

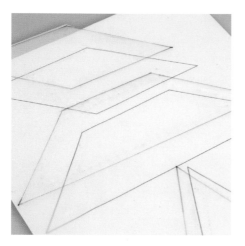

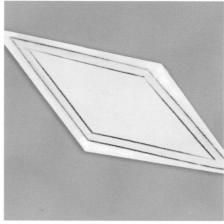

1 Always check to see if the templates include a seam line. If not, photocopy the templates onto copy paper. Trace the shapes onto template plastic using a fine tip marker.

2 Use a rotary cutting ruler to add a 1/4" seam allowance to the outside of the straight sided, traced shapes. I find a 1/2" to 1" x 6" to 12" ruler most useful.

3 Using a pair of scissors, cut directly on the solid line. After cutting, remember to add information to each piece such as name, grain lines or any instructions for that particular shape.

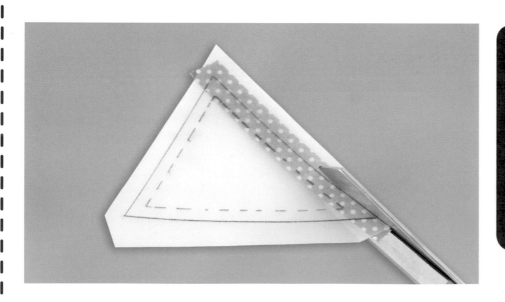

TIP: If you've traced your pattern and it's hard to see the lines on the plastic, place a piece of masking or colored tape behind the line. After you have cut out the template, it's easy to remove the tape from the plastic.

Adding a Seam Allowance to a Template

When a template doesn't include a seam allowance it's the finished size of the piece. But it can easily be added to regular, straight sided shapes. If you want to add a seam allowance to templates that have unusual shapes or curves, it becomes a two-step process.

1 To add a seam allowance to curved shapes cut the template to its finished size using either card stock or template plastic.

2 Place it on template plastic, securing it with double-sided tape to stop it from shifting.

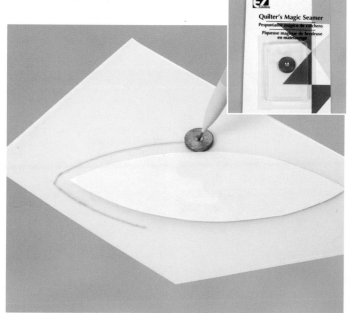

3 Using a "Magic Seam Marker" (see inset), put a pencil in the hole and draw around the shape. The new drawn line will be 1/4" bigger than the original shape.

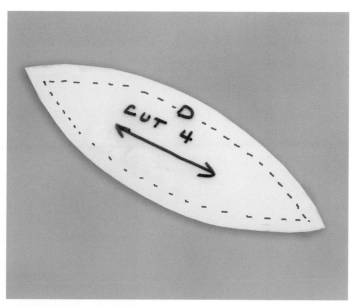

4 Trace the finished size template onto the new template. This line becomes the 1/4" sewing line.

Acrylic Templates

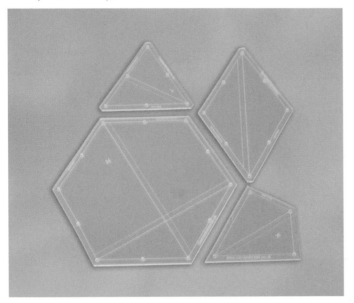

Commercial, acrylic template shapes come in sets for specific patterns and also in general shapes like squares, triangles, diamonds or hexagons. Depending on the maker, some templates will come with the seam allowance lines included or holes in the template to mark a 1/4" seam line on the fabric.

Die Cut Machines

There are several machines on the market and their sole purpose is to reduce the time spent on cutting and creating accurate pieces. They are easy to use and portable. Most dies need to be purchased in addition to the machine. The only limit is whether or not the die shape and size are available for your particular block.

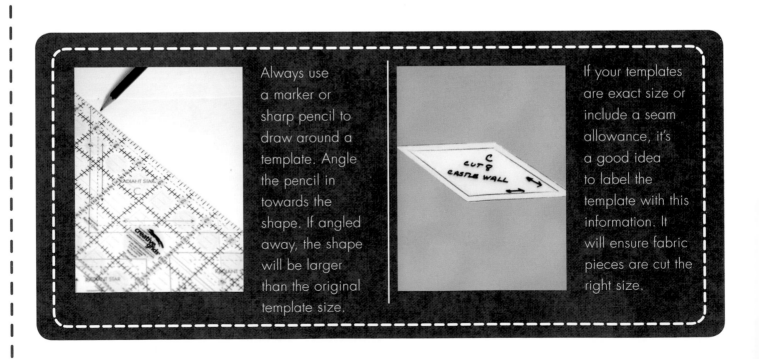

Always use a marker or sharp pencil to draw around a template. Angle the pencil in towards the shape. If angled away, the shape will be larger than the original template size.

If your templates are exact size or include a seam allowance, it's a good idea to label the template with this information. It will ensure fabric pieces are cut the right size.

Cutting Fabric from Templates

Once your templates are prepared and you have made your fabric choices, you will trace and cut the fabric pieces for your blocks. Use a sharp marker and sharp scissors to ensure your pieces are cut correctly. To stabilize your fabric while tracing, use the options below.

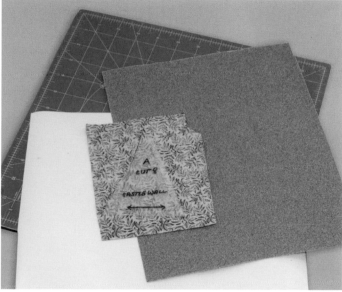

To stabilize your templates on the fabric as you trace around them, try adding sandpaper dots or "Grip Discs" to the back of the template. You can also use repositionable spray glue like 404 that will make the back of the template tacky.

If you don't want to do anything to the templates, try placing your fabric onto a fine sheet of sandpaper. It will grip the fabric and keep it in place. You can also try a rotary mat, Matilda's own Design Mat, or a piece of ROC-LON® Multi-Purpose Cloth™ to place the fabric on while drawing around the template. ROC-LON® has just enough texture to anchor your fabric while tracing.

Just as you did when you drew around template material, make sure to angle your marker in toward the template for the most accuracy.

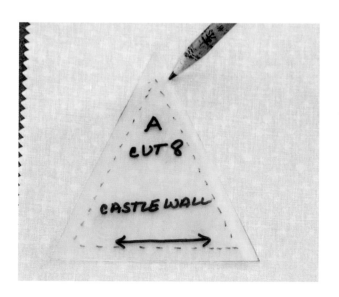

Templates Without a Seam Allowance

If your templates don't include a seam allowance, the following technique will allow you to add it to both straight and curved pieces as you cut your fabric. Using this method means you will always have a sewing line drawn on the back of the fabric, since the traced template is the finished size.

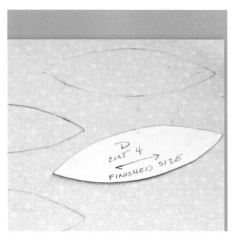

1 On the back of your fabric, trace around the template shape with a sharp marker. This line becomes your stitching line on the back of your fabric.

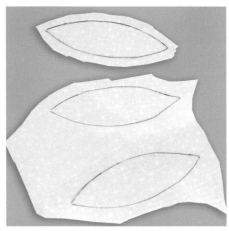

2 Leave enough space between the shapes so you can add 1/4" seam allowance when you cut out the shape.

3 It is better to leave more space than try to be exact. Because you pin and sew on the drawn line, the raw edges of the pieces don't need to line up. If there is more than 1/4" of fabric outside the seam line, you can always trim it. You can't add seam allowance if you cut it too narrow!

Templates with the Seam Allowance Included

When the seam allowance is included on a template you can stack fabric and cut out several pieces at a time. It makes the cutting process faster. It's a good idea to continue drawing the stitching lines on the cut pieces until you become more experienced and need no lines to stitch along.

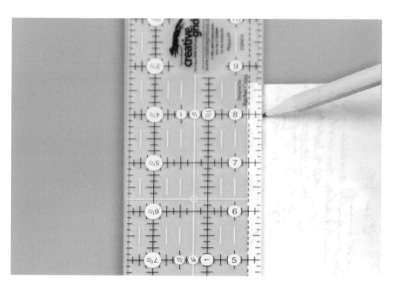

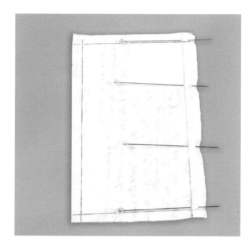

1 If your template shape is straight sided, you may want to add the sewing line to the back of your fabric piece. Place a rotary cutting ruler on the wrong side of your fabric patch and line it up to draw 1/4" in from the raw edge. Mark all sides and corners so you know where to start and stop.

2 It is only necessary to draw on the back of one fabric shape since you will be sewing two pieces, right sides together, and lining up raw edges.

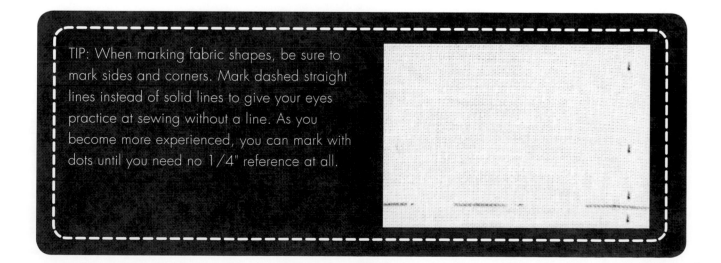

TIP: When marking fabric shapes, be sure to mark sides and corners. Mark dashed straight lines instead of solid lines to give your eyes practice at sewing without a line. As you become more experienced, you can mark with dots until you need no 1/4" reference at all.

Preparing to Stitch

When you are ready to stitch your blocks together, use the previous pages to refer back to if you need help as you stitch. If you are relatively new to hand stitching, layer two pieces of fabric together to practice the basics like stitch length, gathering two or three stitches, and taking backstitches at the beginning, and end on a row of stitches. This will make you more comfortable when you start putting pieces together for your block.

Thread Length

Use your arm to determine a comfortable thread length to stitch with. Hold the thread between your thumb and forefinger, unwind the spool of thread with your other hand and stop at your shoulder. This length will ensure you are using the most comfortable ergonomic action by pulling from the pivot point of your elbow. And this action will create rhythm and consistent tension and stitches.

Threading the Needle

After you have cut your thread, tie a knot in the end you just cut. Thread the free end into the needle. I find it easier to put the needle over the thread than poke the thread into the hole of the needle. Or you may want to use a needle threader like those on page 8.

General Tips for Straight Stitch Sewing

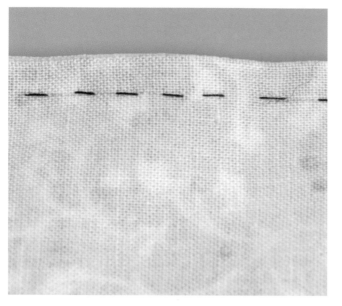

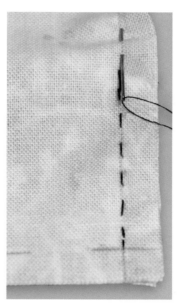

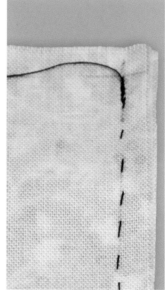

A straight running stitch is a basic stitch. But there are some subtle nuances that may make things easier to create better tension, firmer stitches, and consistent stitch length.

To start, stitch with a backstitch at the knotted end. When you come to the finish, end with two or three backstitches.

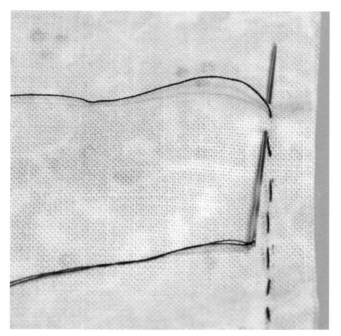

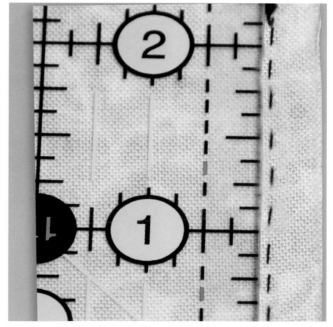

It isn't the quantity but the quality of the stitches. Stitch quality comes with practice. They need to be firm so if you pull the seam open, you cannot see daylight through the gaps. Taking a backstitch every inch or so will contribute to good tension and act as a lock to stop stitches from unraveling.

The question often comes up concerning number of stitches per inch. I have never really worried about it but in order to answer the question, I counted my stitches on several projects I've made. I stitch roughly nine stitches per inch, which means I have five on the top and four on the bottom. This can vary, depending on fabric and thread thickness.

Sewing A Firm Seam

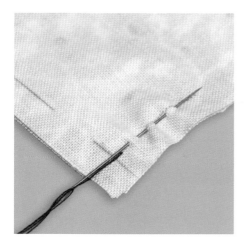

As you sew, you pick up and pull the thread through for a stitch. You can gather up two, three or four stitches and send your needle through the fabric and pull. Remember to take a backstitch every inch or so.

When you are sewing a long seam, it's easier to sew if your fabric is under tension. There are several tools to add tension to your fabric. A "Sewing Bird" is a decorative clamp from Victorian times that is secured to a table edge. The mouth of the bird holds the end of the seam while stitching, pulling it tight. Sewing Birds are still available but you can always improvise this tension in other ways.

Use heavy duty clamps big enough to span the thickness of your table or desk. They will hold your fabric in the same way as a "Sewing Bird".

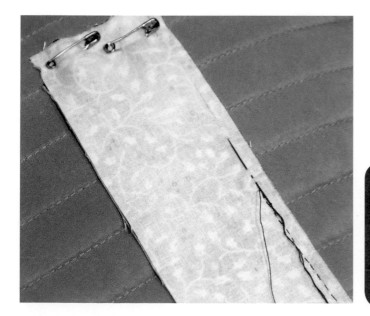

Another way to improvise tension in the seam is to pin the end of the piece to a pillow on your lap. Stitch in either direction from the pins, whichever is more comfortable. Gently pull against the pins to add the tension.

Tip: If you are stitching at a desk or table, hold the end of the pieces down on the table top with the hand that holds your needle. The pressure/weight from your hand creates a natural tension. Move your patches forward as you continue to stitch.

Keepers & Pincushions

The projects that follow are quick and easy ways to organize your block pieces and keep pins handy as you pin pieces ready to sew.

Block Keeper Roll

It's a nice idea to store your blocks as you stitch them. A large, flat storage box is handy, but if you are out and about with your work, then a cumbersome box might not be the only solution. In minutes, you can make a keeper to roll and store your blocks.

Quick Block Roll

MATERIALS:

(1) 20" cardboard tube 2" in diameter

(1) yard ribbon

(1) 3/4" button

(1) 18-1/2" x 28" tea towel

OR

5/8 yard fabric. Choose linen or a heavier weight cotton for body.

18" x 28" piece of batting, felt, or flannel to line tea towel or fabric piece

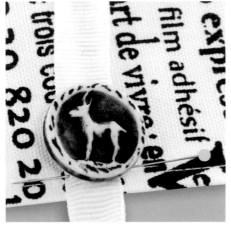

1 If you are using fabric, cut a piece 20" x 30" and double hem all four sides. If you are using a tea towel, all sides are hemmed for you. Find the middle of one of the short sides and mark with a pin or marking pencil. Fold the ribbon in half, place on the right side of fabric where the center is marked.

2 Place the button on top of ribbon and stitch in place through the ribbon and fabric.

3 Place the batting on the inside of the fabric roll. Lay block pieces or finished block on the batting, span the cardboard tube along the short side, roll and tie to close.

Finger Pincushion

MATERIALS:

(1) 4-1/2" fabric square

thread to blend with fabric

batting

A very small, really useful item for a hand-piecer is a little pin cushion that can be worn on a finger while stitching. If you start using one when you stitch, you will find them indispensable.

Here's how quickly you can stitch one, either by hand or machine.

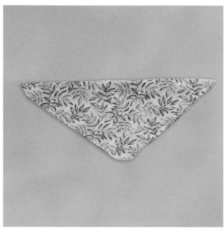

1 Fold the square in half diagonally with right sides together. Stitch a 1/4" seam around raw edges, leaving a 1" opening in a side.

2 Trim each corner and turn right side out.

3 Gently stuff with batting until firm. Do not overstuff or you won't be able to fold into a ring. Understuffing will make the cushion too flat and you may prick yourself with pins.

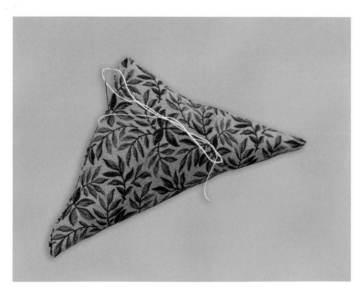

4 Stitch the cushion closed.

5 Fold triangle points to meet and overlap by about 1/2". Stitch through all layers firmly to keep the ring together.

Stitching Pieces

Stitching the Pieces Together

All the blocks in the quilt can be sewn with the following techniques. Some blocks, like a four patch, are just straight stitching. Other blocks combine simple stitching and combinations of other techniques. It is good practice to start with two patches and working through to stitching eight patches together. That way, there are no surprises when you start making the blocks!

Pinning into the seam allowance will help you see what the seam will look like before you stitch it. It may not be so important on a straight seam, but on seams with more pieces it will help you see how accurate you are before you begin stitching.

Stitching Two Patches Together

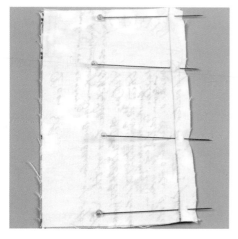

1 Pin the two patches together at the start and finish and in between as necessary. Pin on the sewing line and into the seam allowance. This will help you see what the seam will look like before you stitch it.

2 Thread a needle with a length of toning thread (I used a contrasting thread for easy visibility), and knot end. Remove first pin and insert the needle on the corner to make the first stitch and then a backstitch.

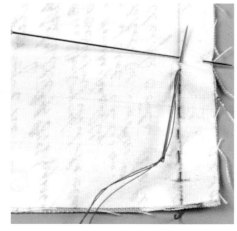

3 Continue along the sewing line and make a backstitch about every inch of stitching. Remove pins as you sew.

Note: Backstitching at every inch or so will stop the thread from gathering up if it gets pulled and it will give your seam nice tension.

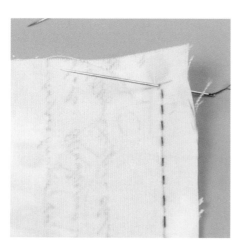

4 When you reach the end of the seam bring the needle up from the back where the last pin sits at the corner.

5 Make three backstitches back along the sewn seam.

6 Snip the thread, leaving a tail of about 1". This will give you some thread insurance if the seam gets pulled. Your stitches may start to unravel if the thread is cut very close to the seam.

Stitching Three Patches Together

When stitching more than two pieces together, it makes it easier if you don't sew down the seam allowance in any one position. Pressing the seam allowance is done when the work is finished. I have approached this by placing the joins of the sewn patches facing me as I sew. I can see the seam allowance and keep from sewing it down. As you become used to the process, you can work with the joins on the back.

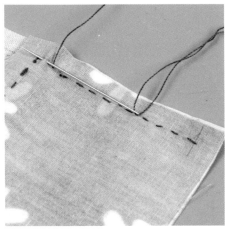

1 Layering the pieces, making sure that the two sewn patches are on the front of your work so you can see the seam. This will make it easier to approach and skip over the sewn seam.

2 Pin right sides together on the sewing line and into the seam allowance.

3 Start stitching at the corner and progress towards the upright seam. Push the upright seam allowance away from the seam you are sewing.

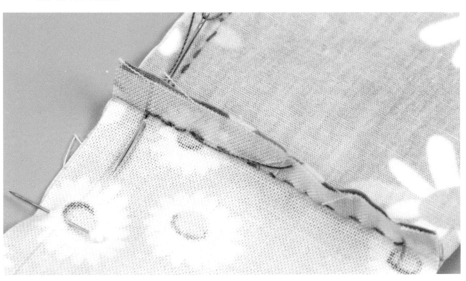

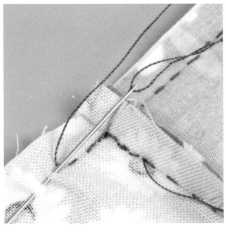

4 When you reach the seam, push the needle to the back and come up on the other side of the upright seam one stitch ahead of the corner. Make sure there is no seam allowance in the needle. Take a backstitch.

5 After skipping the upright seam, this backstitch will lock the stitches and stop the stitches from gaping. Continue on to the end of the seam as usual.

Stitching Four and Six Patches Together

When you sew four patches together you will have seams that match up with upright seam allowances on the front and back of your work. Neither of the upright seams should be sewn down. By following these steps you will have a nice, concise join.

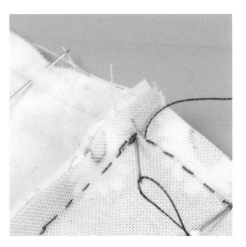

1 Pin two sets of patches right sides together along the seam line and into the seam allowance. Push the two previously sewn seams away from the direction you are sewing.

2 Start stitching on the corner, taking a backstitch, and sew toward the upright seam of sewn patch.

3 As you approach the junction of the upright seam with the last stitch, push the needle through at a diagonal, keeping the seam allowance on the front pushed back toward the sewn seam and the bottom seam allowance pushed away from the sewn seam.

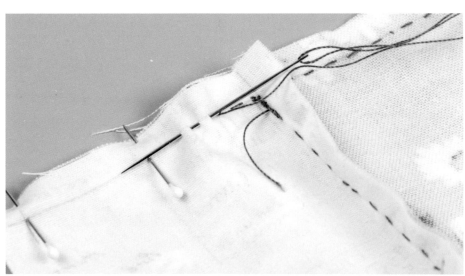

4 The needle should come up ahead of the corner on the back of the work, ready to take a backstitch.

5 By taking a backstitch and pulling tight, the junction of the four seams will not gape. Continue to the end of the patch and finish with three backstitches along the seam line.

Stitching Set-In Seams

Blocks like the Friends All Around or Spools block are made up of straight sewing but some of the seams will need to be set-in, or "sewn around the corner". This is also referred to as a "Y" seam. One of the lovely things about hand-sewn patchwork is the ease with which these "obstacles" can be dealt with. The following instructions use the Spools block to show how to set in pieces.

"Y" or "set-in" seams are similar to stitching three patches together. You will stitch a pre-sewn set of pieces to a piece with no seams. But now, several seams are sewn on an angle. Set-in seams are pinned and sewn in separate stages, one at a time.

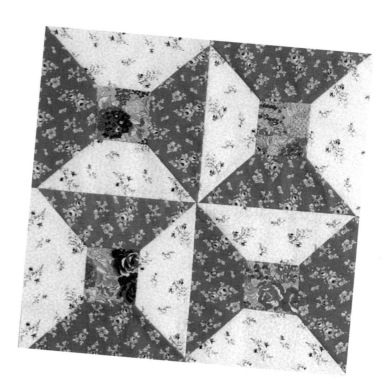

1 For this technique, the pieces from the Spools block are used for the step-by-step. The first three pieces are sewn together, ready to attach pieces with set-in corners.

2 With right sides together, pin the next section along the sewing line and into the seam allowance. (You can use your needle as the first pin). The unsewn piece is on the front in this instance and sewn pieces with seams are on the back. Push the previously sewn seam away so you do not pin it down.

3 Start stitching on the point, taking a backstitch. Remove the pins as you sew and stitch until you reach the 1/4" seam line at the first corner. Finish with a backstitch.

4 Realign the edges of your fabric piece to "turn a corner".

5 Pin to the next corner, pushing the seam allowance away on the back. Start with a backstitch and stitch along the seam line to the last corner and take a backstitch.

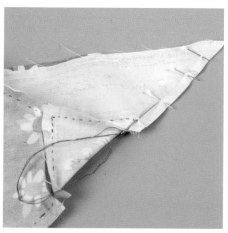  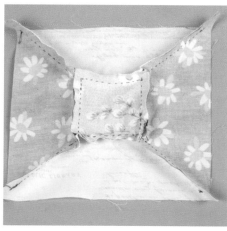

6 Realign and pin the edges of your fabric piece to "turn the corner". Push your needle through to the back, jumping the seam allowance, and bring it up one stitch from the other side of the corner. Take a backstitch. There should be no stitch in the seam allowance.

7 Stitch to the end of the seam and finish with three backstitches to complete the set-in seam.

8 Repeat steps 2-7 to complete the Spools block.

Stitching Curves

As you know, not all patchwork is made up of straight line piecing. Sewing curves opens up a whole new variety of patchwork designs. These basic instructions will get you started sewing the curves that make up some of the blocks in this book.

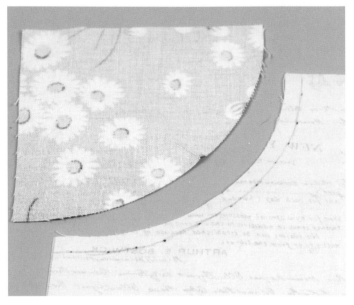

1 Transfer any marks from the templates to the wrong side of the fabric along the seam line. Here, I have finger pressed the center of the pieces by folding them in half.

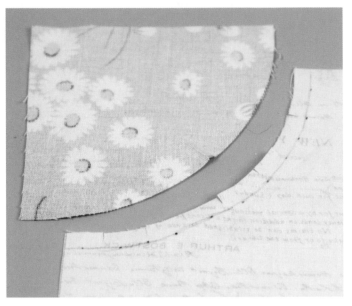

2 Depending on the tightness of the curve, you may wish to snip 1/8" on either or both of the two patches. Here, I have snipped along the concave piece.

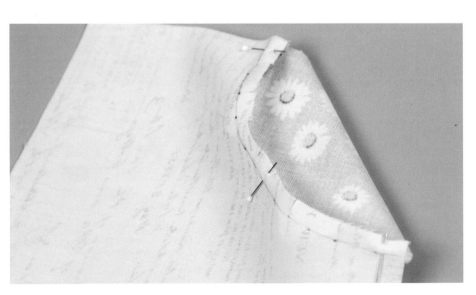

3 Pin the pieces, right sides together along the seam line matching finger pressed centers. Start at either end or in the middle.

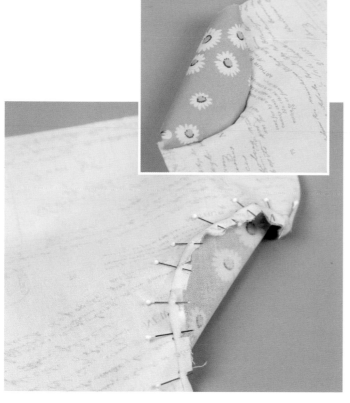

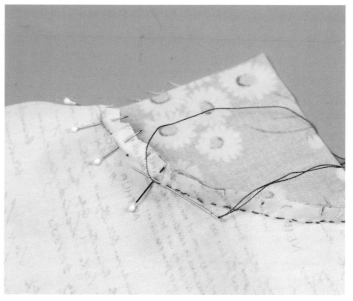

4 Pin along the entire seam between the pins to accommodate any fullness. Open to the right side to see if seam lies flat (see inset). If the seam needs adjusting, do that now before sewing.

5 Start stitching, taking a backstitch, and continue as you would for a straight seam. Remove pins as you sew and add a backstitch every inch or so.

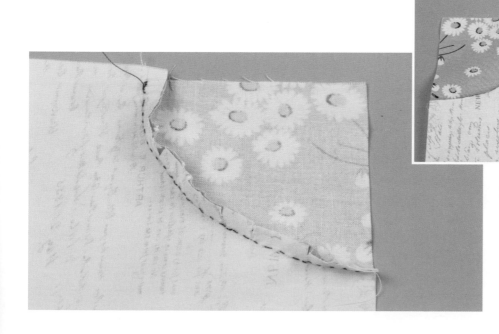

6 Continue to the end of the patch and finish with three backstitches along the seam line.

Stitching Eight Patches Together

The Le Moyne Star block has eight pieces that are sewn in sections to make a star. This technique can also be used to make a six pointed star.

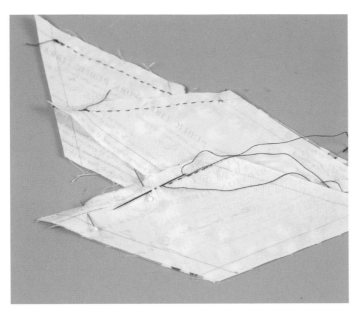

1 Referring to Stitching Two Patches, page 27, sew the diamonds together in pairs.

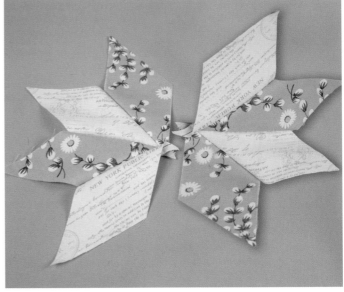

2 An eight-pointed star is sewn with two pairs of diamonds to make half a star. Stitch two sets of four diamonds to make a star.

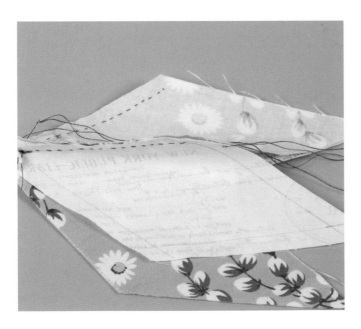

3 Pin the two halves together. Pin so that the seams in the center are pushed out of the way. Stitch the seam and take a backstitch at the center, making sure no seam allowances are in the stitch.

4 Reinsert the needle diagonally across the junction, ahead of the start of the stitch line on the back. Pull the thread tight and take a backstitch to ensure the junction will not gape. Continue sewing the seam and finish with three backstitches along the seam line.

5 Press all the seams in the same direction.

6 There should be no stitches through any of the seam allowances at the center junction. The points in the center should spiral and lay flat, revealing a second, secret star.

7 This star will be completed using the Stitching Set-In Seams technique, page 30.

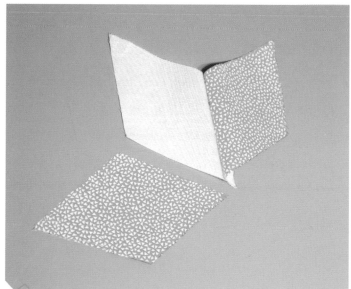

8 For a six-pointed star, sew a remaining diamond to a pair to make half a star. Repeat for the second half. Make sure the seams where the diamonds come together are tight where the points meet. Repeat steps 3-5 to finish a six-pointed star.

Stitching the Blocks

Remember that you do not need to press the block until it is complete, and that sometimes the pressing will vary depending on the handle of the fabric. Unlike machine-sewn patchwork, where the pressing is an integral part of sewing the block, it is not with hand-pieced patchwork. This is because we do not sew through the seam allowance so it doesn't have to be in a particular position in order for the next part of the process to be complete.

Remember to check the basics section of hand piecing (pages 18-35) for hints and suggestions on things you might want to try now that you're sewing the blocks.

The blocks over the following pages are in order of ease of stitching. You can dip in and out and stitch the blocks in any order you like, but if you have not sewn much patchwork by hand then you might want to build up your skill level by starting with the easiest blocks.

Each block will show the templates needed, the order of stitching, photo of suggested pressing, and unfinished block size.

IMPORTANT:
SEAM ALLOWANCE IS INCLUDED IN EVERY TEMPLATE.

ARROWS ON THE TEMPLATES INDICATE STRAIGHT OF GRAIN.

Blocks in Order of Skill Level:

1. Rectangles

2. Squares,
2, 4 & 6 Patch

3. Half-Square
Triangles

4. Quarter-Square Triangles

5. Shoo Fly

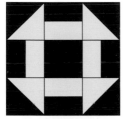
6. Churn Dash

7. Flying Geese

8. 16 Patch Sawtooth Star

9. Radiant Star

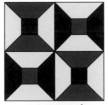
10. Spools

11. Amish Star

12. Mayflower   13. Le Moyne Star

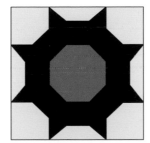
14. Castle Wall

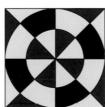
15. Millwheel

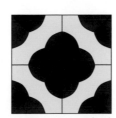
16. Signature Block

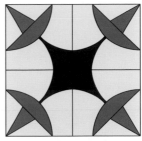
17. Turkey Tracks

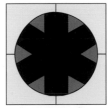
18. Pieced Sunflower

19. Lily of the Valley

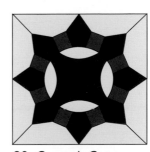
20. Caesar's Crown

21. Hands All Around

Rectangles—Chinese Coins

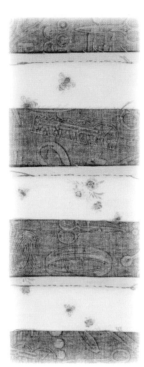
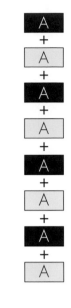

Cutting

From the LIGHT fabric, cut:

(9)   A pieces

From the DARK fabric, cut:

(9)   A pieces

Stitching Techniques

Refer to page 27,
Stitching Two Pieces Together

Press seams as shown.

1

2

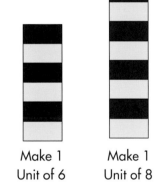

Make 1
Unit of 6

Make 1
Unit of 8

Make 1
Unit of 4
for Border

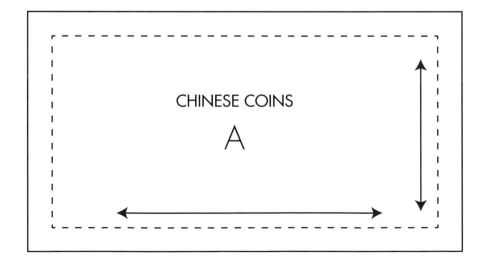

CHINESE COINS

A

Squares—2, 4 & 6 Patch

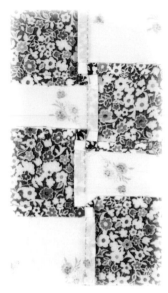

Cutting

From the LIGHT fabric, cut:
(22) A pieces

From the DARK fabric, cut:
(22) A pieces

Stitching Techniques

Refer to page 27,
Stitching Two Pieces Together

Press seams as shown.

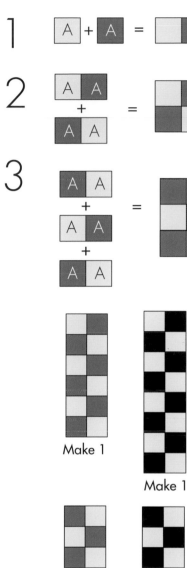

1 A + A = ▢▪

2 A A
   +   = ▢▪
   A A   ▪▢

3 A A
   +
   A A   = [6 patch]
   +
   A A

Make 1

Make 1

Make 1
for border

Make 1
for border

Set aside:
(1) 2 patch for Caesar's
Crown Section 6

2, 4 & 6 PATCH

A

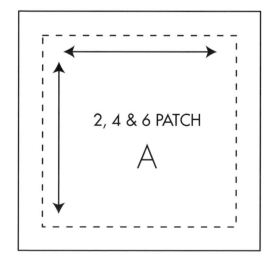

Half-Square Triangles

1

2

Make 1 Unit

Cutting

From the LIGHT fabric, cut:
(3)   A pieces

From the DARK fabric, cut:
(3)   A pieces

Stitching Techniques

Refer to page 20,
Straight Running Stitch

Press seams as shown.

HALF-SQUARE
TRIANGLES

A

Quarter-Square Triangles

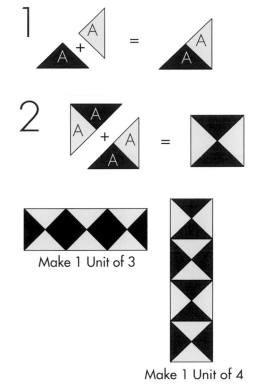

Make 1 Unit of 3

Make 1 Unit of 4

Cutting

From the LIGHT fabric, cut:
(14) A pieces

From the DARK fabric, cut:
(14) A pieces

Stitching Techniques

Refer to page 27,
Stitching Two Pieces Together

Press seams as shown.

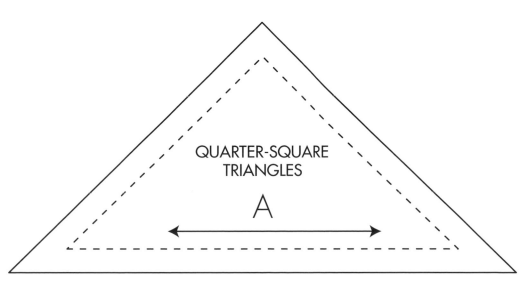

QUARTER-SQUARE
TRIANGLES

A

Shoo Fly

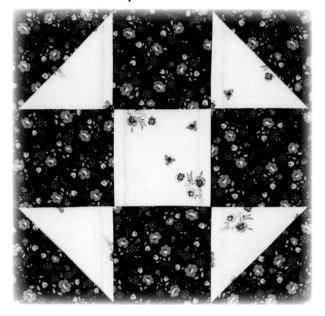

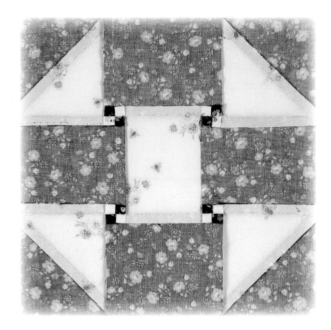

Cutting

From the LIGHT fabric, cut:

(1)   B piece

(4)   A pieces

From the DARK fabric, cut:

(4)   B pieces

(4)   A pieces

Stitching Techniques

Refer to page 27,
Stitching Two Pieces Together

Press seams as shown.

1

2

3

4

5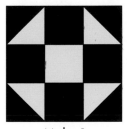

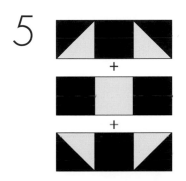

Make 1
9-1/2" Block

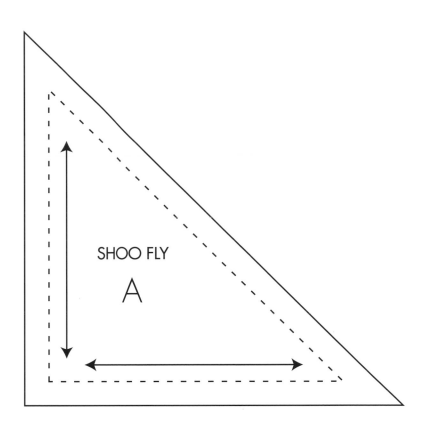

SHOO FLY

A

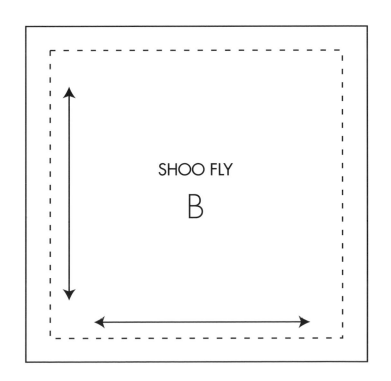

SHOO FLY

B

Churn Dash

Cutting

From the LIGHT fabric, cut:

(16) A pieces

(2)   C pieces

(16) B pieces

From the DARK fabric, cut:

(16) A pieces

(2)   C pieces

(16) B pieces

Stitching Techniques

Refer to page 27,
Stitching Two Pieces Together

Press seams as shown.

1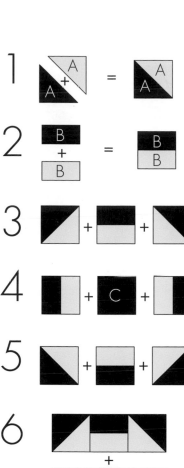

2

3

4

5

6

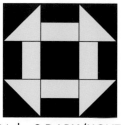 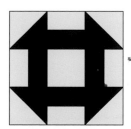

Make 2 DARK/LIGHT
9-1/2" Blocks

Make 2 LIGHT/DARK
9-1/2" Blocks

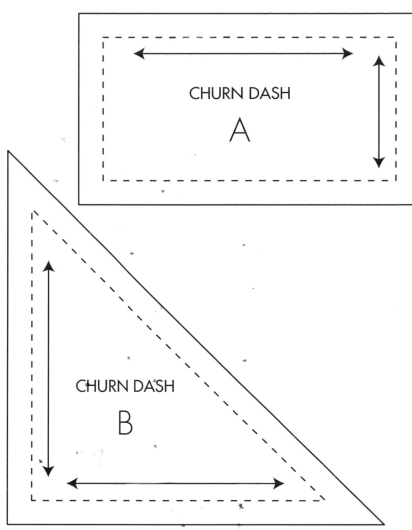

CHURN DASH

A

CHURN DASH

B

CHURN DASH

C

Flying Geese

Cutting

From the LIGHT fabric, cut:
(16) B pieces

From the DARK fabric, cut:
(32) A pieces

Stitching Techniques

Refer to page 20,
Straight Running Stitch

Press seams as shown.

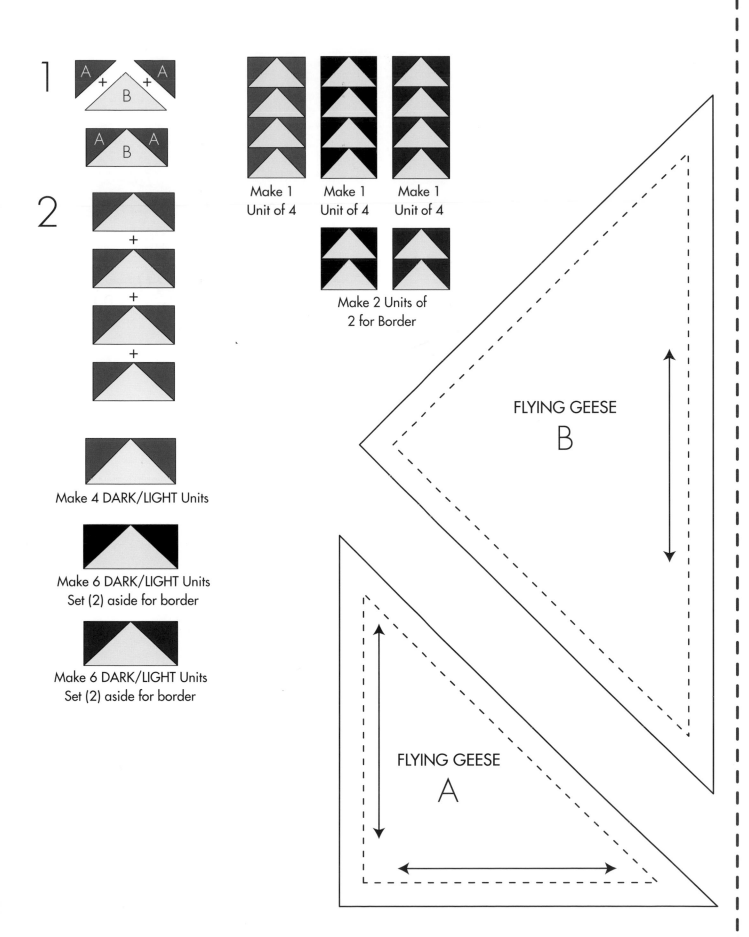

1

2

Make 4 DARK/LIGHT Units

Make 6 DARK/LIGHT Units
Set (2) aside for border

Make 6 DARK/LIGHT Units
Set (2) aside for border

Make 1
Unit of 4

Make 1
Unit of 4

Make 1
Unit of 4

Make 2 Units of
2 for Border

FLYING GEESE
B

FLYING GEESE
A

16 Patch Star

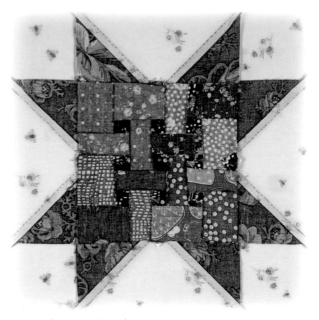

Cutting

From the LIGHT fabric, cut:

(4)   A pieces

(4)   B pieces

From the DARK fabric, cut:

(16)   C pieces

(8)   D pieces

Stitching Techniques

Refer to page 20,
Straight Running Stitch

Press seams as shown.

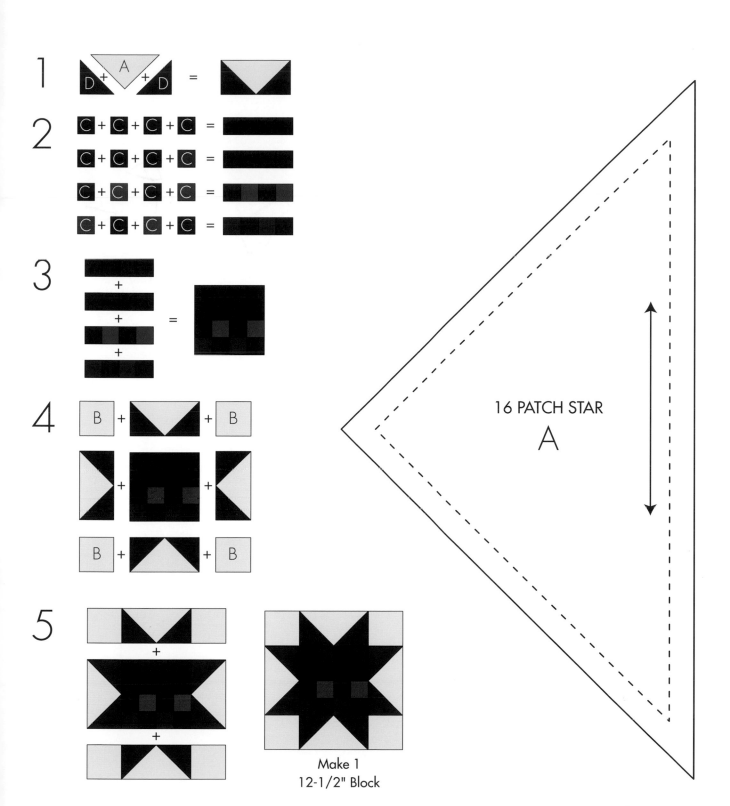

1

2

3

4

5

Make 1
12-1/2" Block

16 PATCH STAR
A

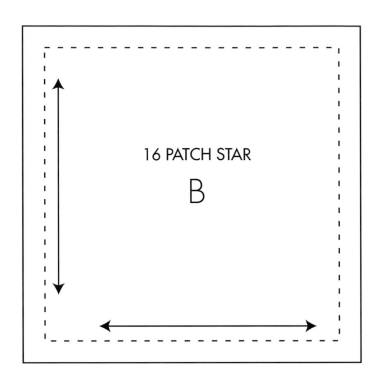

16 PATCH STAR

B

16 PATCH STAR

C

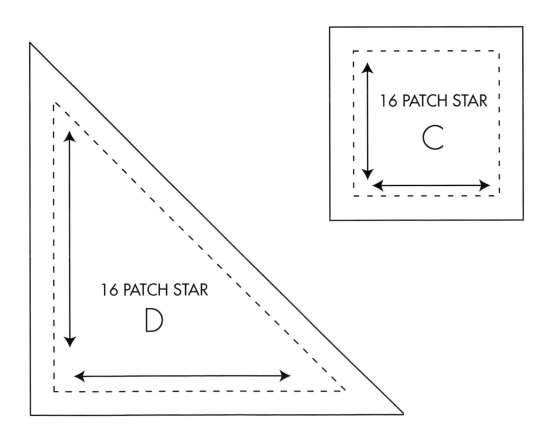

16 PATCH STAR

D

Radiant Star

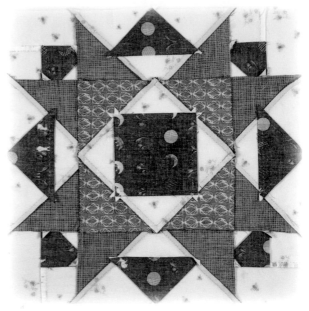

Cutting

From the LIGHT fabric, cut:

(16) B pieces

(4) D pieces

(4) E pieces

(4) F pieces

From the DARK fabric, cut:

(1) A piece

(4) F pieces

(12) C pieces

(4) B pieces

Stitching Techniques

Refer to page 20,
Straight Running Stitch

Refer to pages 27 & 29,
Stitching 2, 4 & 6 Pieces Together

Press seams as shown.

1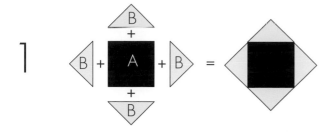

2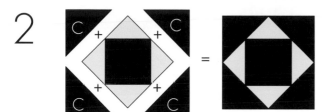

3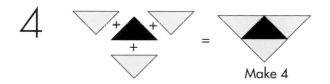

Make 4

4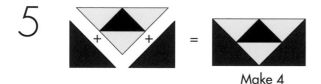

Make 4

5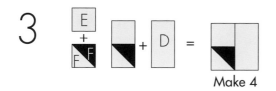

Make 4

6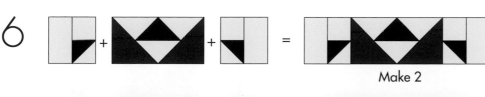

Make 2

7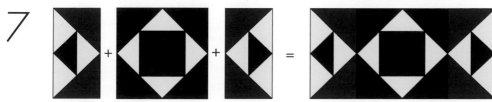

8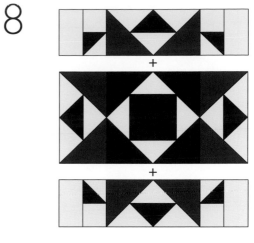

Make 1
16-1/2" Block

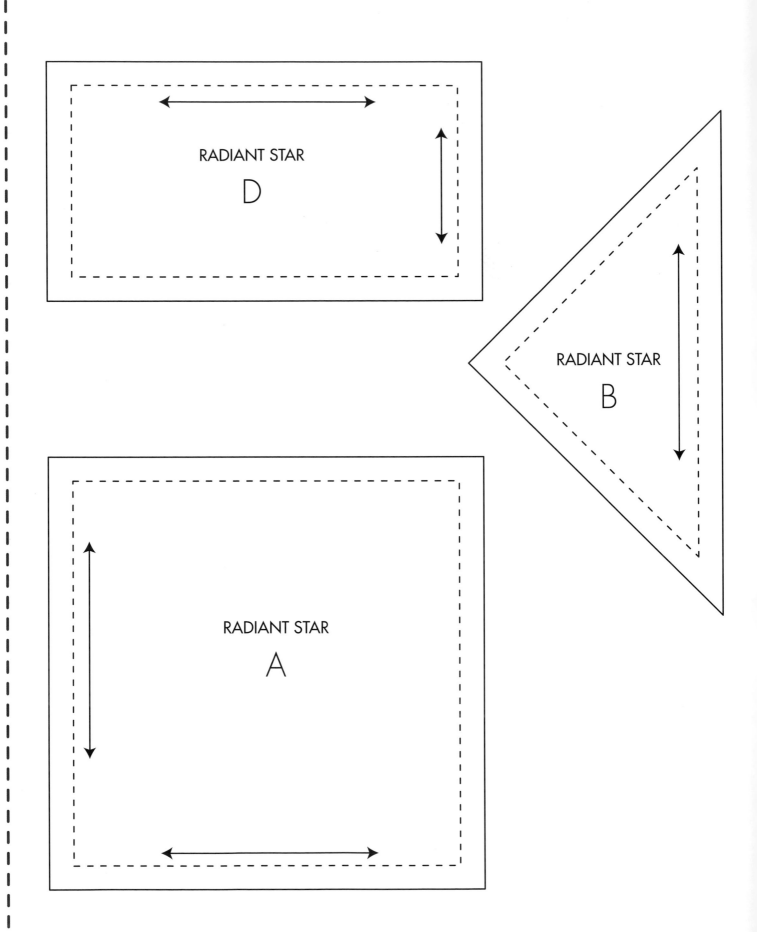

RADIANT STAR

D

RADIANT STAR

B

RADIANT STAR

A

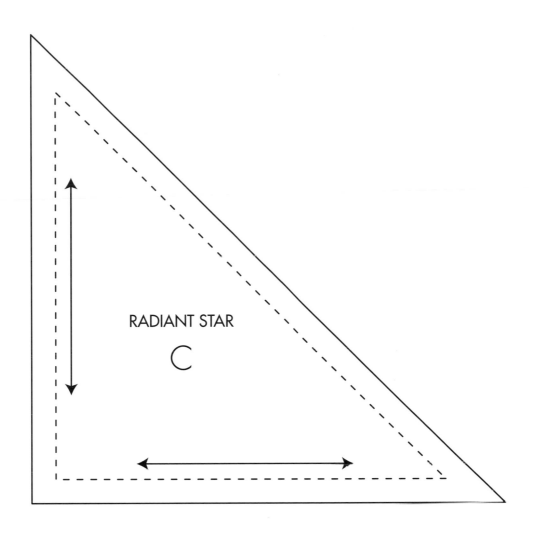

RADIANT STAR

C

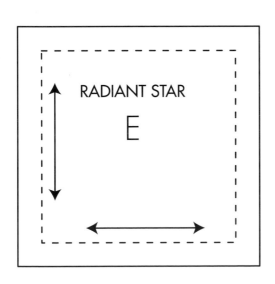

RADIANT STAR

E

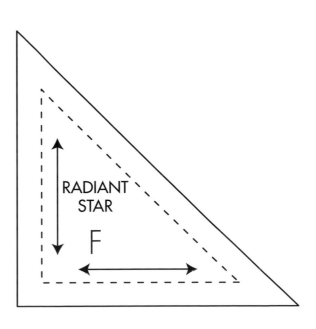

RADIANT STAR

F

Spools

Cutting

From the LIGHT fabric, cut:

(8)   B pieces

From the DARK fabric, cut:

(8)   B pieces

(4)   A pieces

Stitching Techniques

Refer to page 20,
Straight Running Stitch

Refer to page 30,
Stitching Set-In Seams

Press seams as shown.

1

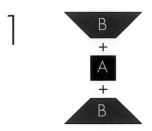

2

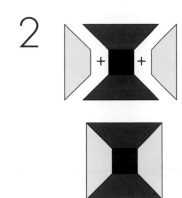

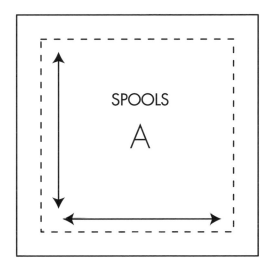

Make 4

Make 1
12-1/2" Block

SPOOLS

A

SPOOLS

B

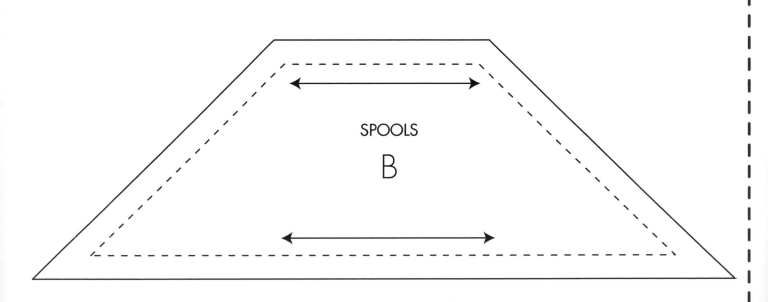

Amish Star

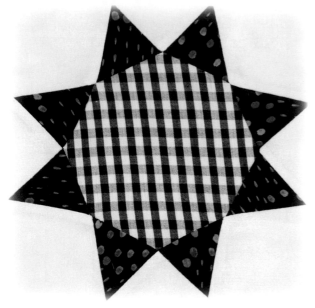 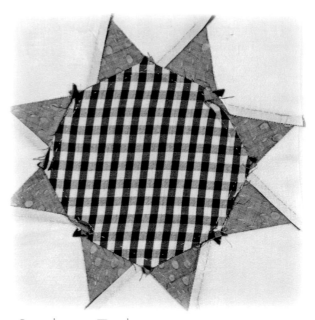

Cutting

From the LIGHT fabric, cut:

(4)   C pieces

(2)   D pieces

(2)   D pieces reversed

From the DARK fabric, cut:

(1)   A piece

(4)   B pieces

(4)   B pieces reversed

Stitching Techniques

Refer to page 30,
Stitching Set-In Seams

Press seams as shown.

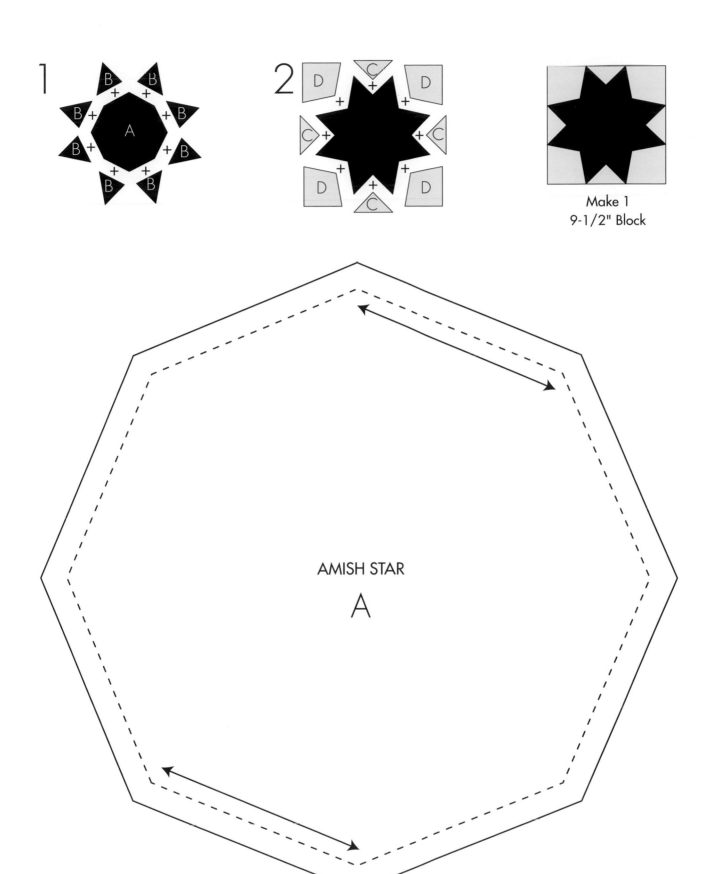

1

B + B
B +   + B
B + A + B
B +   + B
B + B

2

D   C   D
    + + +
C +   + C
    + + +
D   C   D

Make 1
9-1/2" Block

AMISH STAR

A

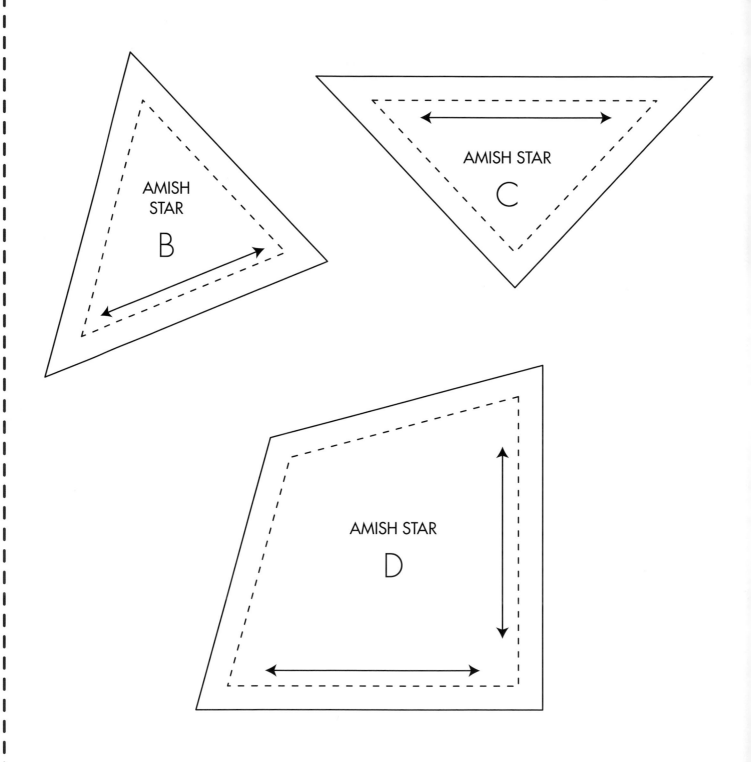

AMISH STAR

B

AMISH STAR

C

AMISH STAR

D

Mayflower

Cutting

From the LIGHT fabric, cut:

(12) B pieces

(12) C pieces

From the DARK fabric, cut:

(12) A pieces

Stitching Techniques

Refer to page 20,
Straight Running Stitch

Refer to page 30,
Stitching Set-In Seams

Press seams as shown.

1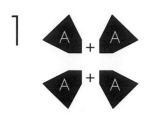

2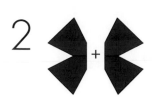

3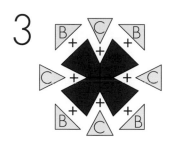

Make 1 Unit of 2
6-1/2" Blocks

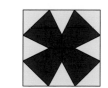

Make 1 Unit for Border
6-1/2" Block

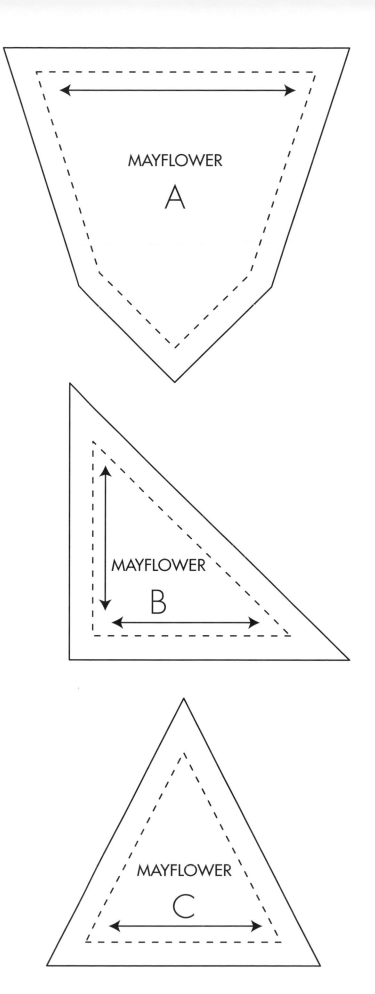

MAYFLOWER

A

MAYFLOWER

B

MAYFLOWER

C

Le Moyne Star

Cutting

From the LIGHT fabric, cut:

(16) B pieces

(16) C pieces

From the DARK fabric, cut:

(32) A pieces

Stitching Techniques

Refer to page 20,
Straight Running Stitch

Refer to page 30,
Stitching Set-In Seams

Press seams as shown.

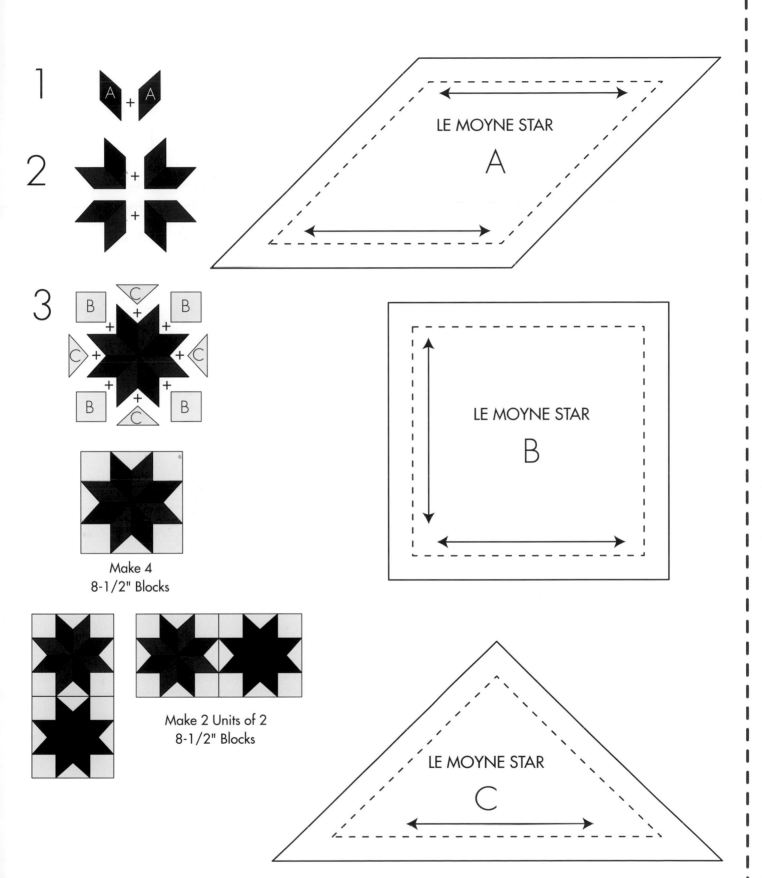

1

2

3

Make 4
8-1/2" Blocks

Make 2 Units of 2
8-1/2" Blocks

LE MOYNE STAR

A

LE MOYNE STAR

B

LE MOYNE STAR

C

Castle Wall

From the LIGHT fabric, cut:

(4)   G pieces

From the DARK fabric, cut:

(8)   B pieces

(8)   C pieces

(1)   A piece

NOTE: G can be made by
combining E and D.
Another color could be
added to the block by
combining these pieces.

To make (4) DE pieces, cut:

(4)   D pieces

(4)   E pieces

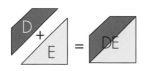

Stitching Techniques

Refer to page 20,
Straight Running Stitches

Refer to page 30,
Stitching Set-In Seams

Press seams as shown.

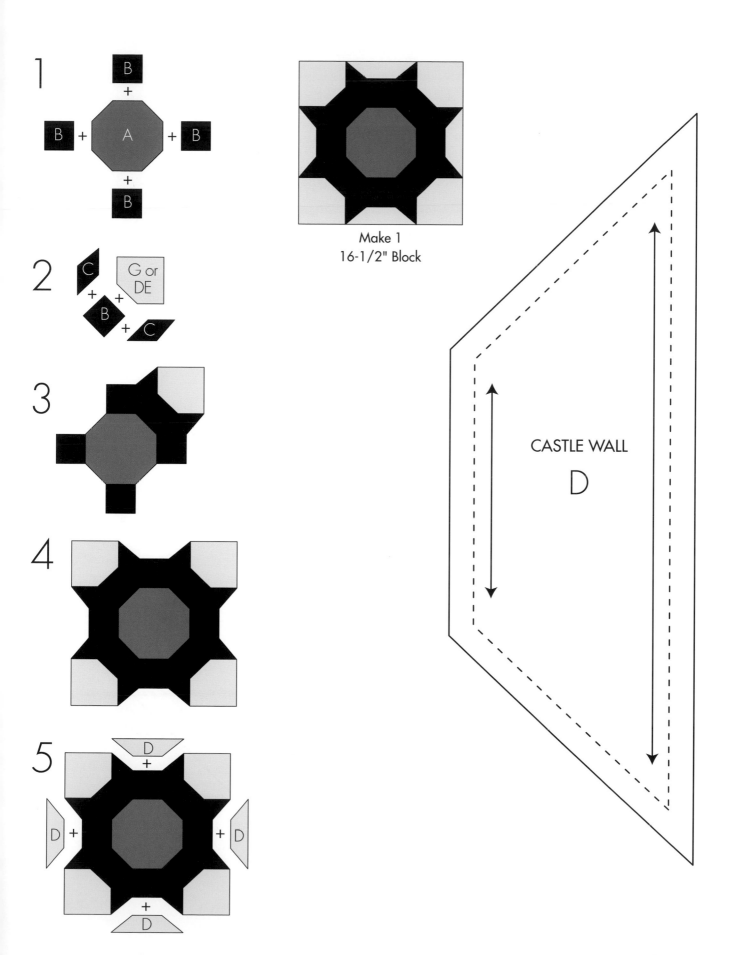

1

B

+

B + A + B

+

B

2

C G or DE

+ +

B

+ C

3

4

5

D

+

D + + D

+

D

Make 1
16-1/2" Block

CASTLE WALL
D

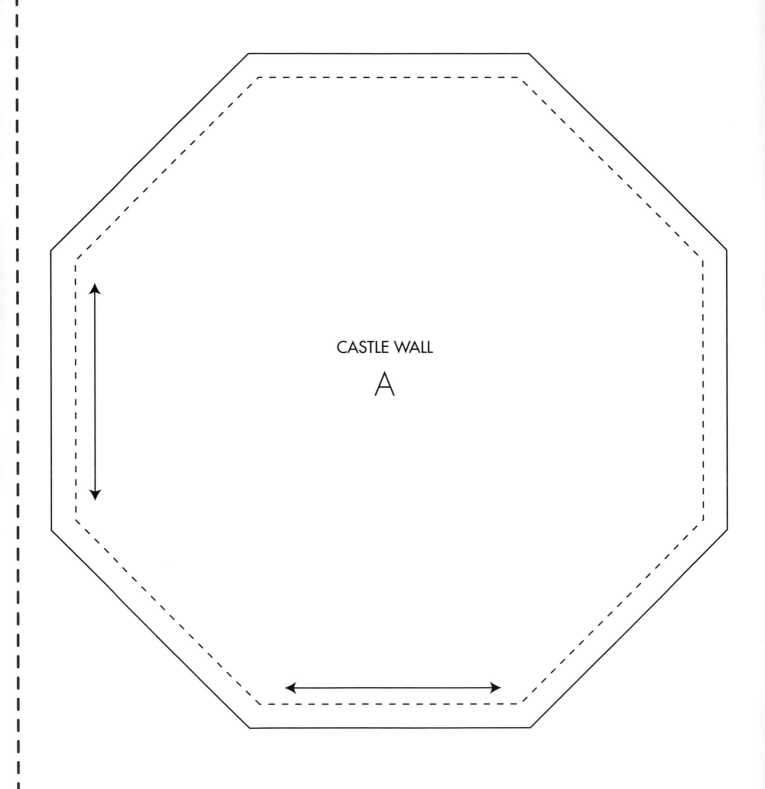

CASTLE WALL

A

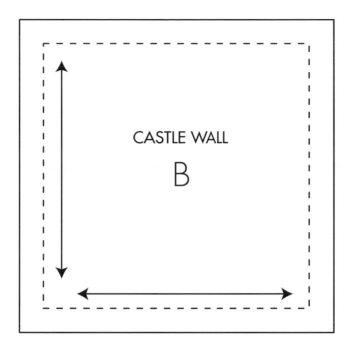

CASTLE WALL

B

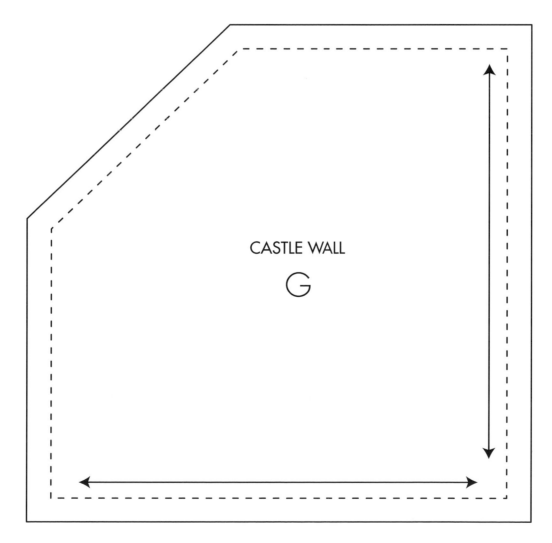

CASTLE WALL

G

If desired, use the D Template on page 67 and the E Template to make the G Template. See page 69..

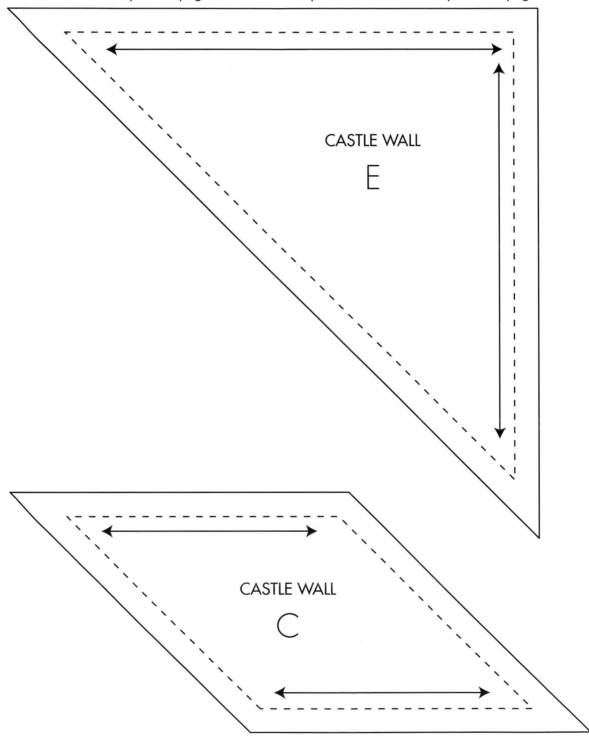

CASTLE WALL

E

CASTLE WALL

C

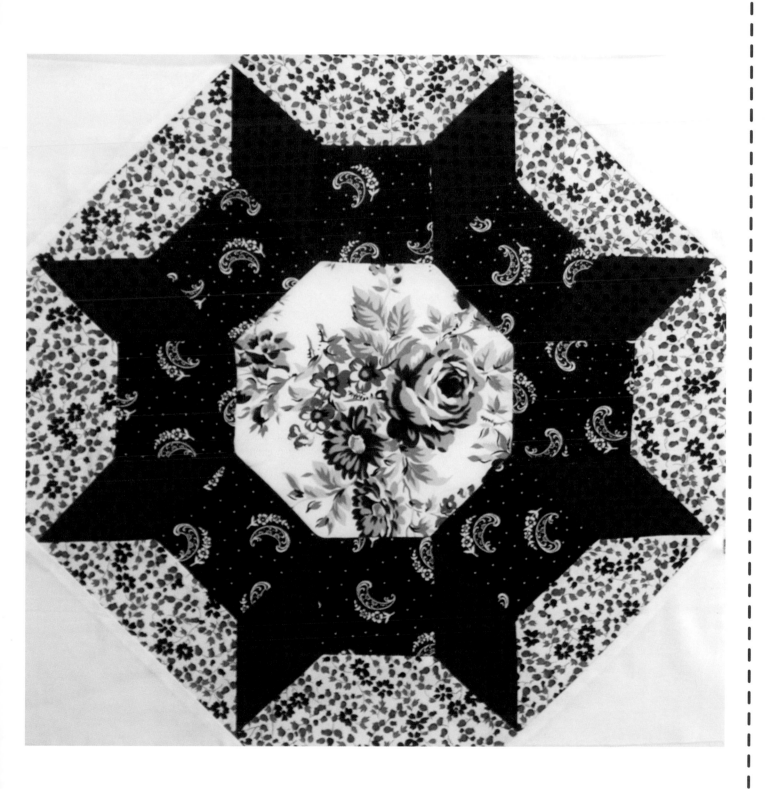

Millwheel

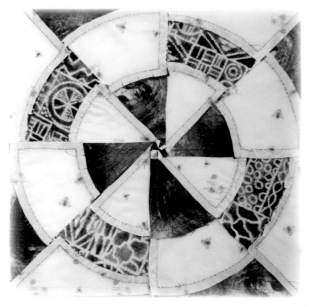

Cutting

From the LIGHT fabric, cut:

(4)   A pieces

(4)   B pieces

(4)   C pieces

From the DARK fabric, cut:

(4)   A pieces

(4)   B pieces

(4)   C pieces

Stitching Techniques

Refer to page 20,
Straight Running Stitch

Refer to page 34,
Stitching Curves

Press seams as shown.

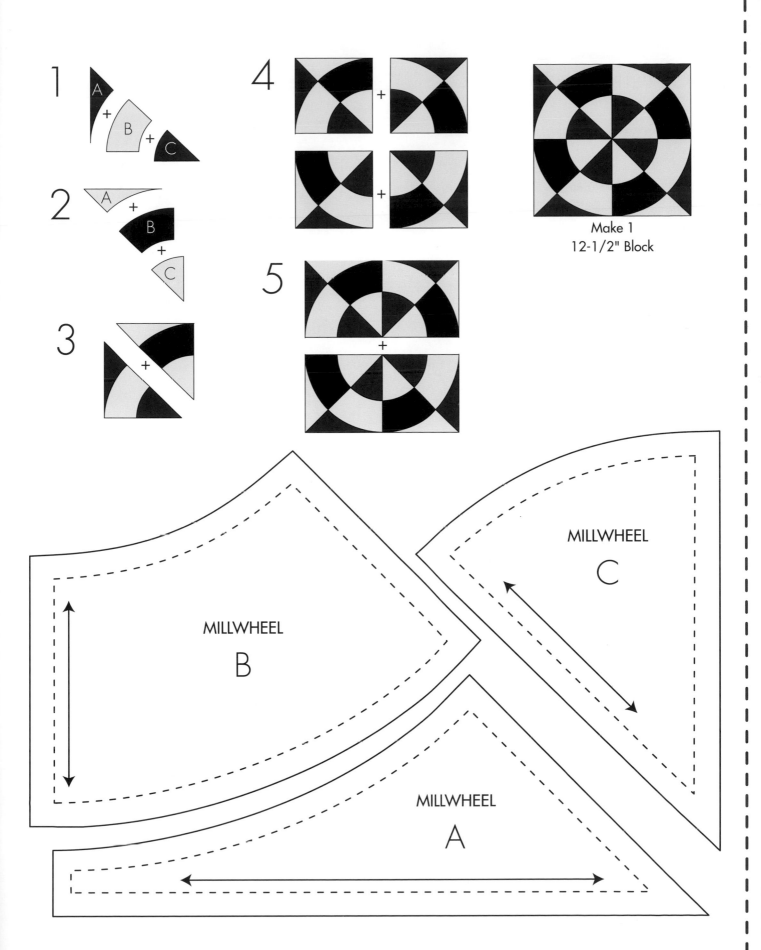

1

2

3

4

5

Make 1
12-1/2" Block

MILLWHEEL
B

MILLWHEEL
C

MILLWHEEL
A

Signature Block

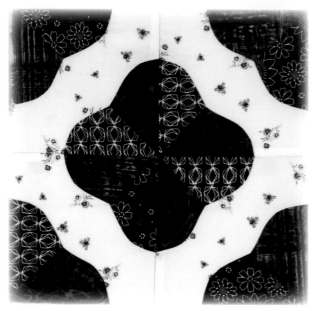
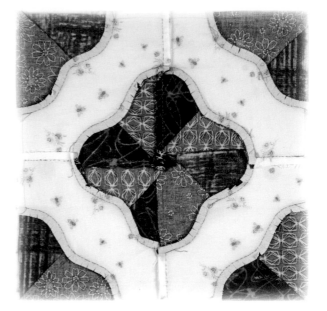

Cutting

From the LIGHT fabric, cut:

(4) A pieces

From the DARK fabric, cut:

(8) B pieces

(8) B pieces reversed

Stitching Techniques

Refer to page 20,
Straight Running Stitch

Refer to page 34,
Stitching Curves

Press seams as shown.

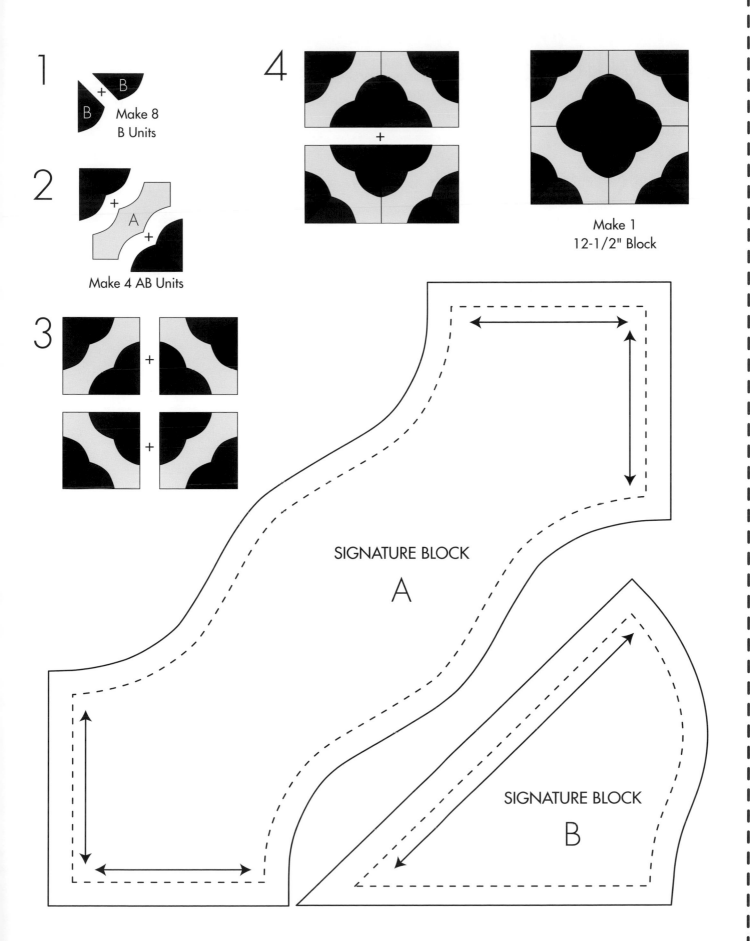

1 Make 8
B Units

2 Make 4 AB Units

3

4

Make 1
12-1/2" Block

SIGNATURE BLOCK
A

SIGNATURE BLOCK
B

Turkey Tracks

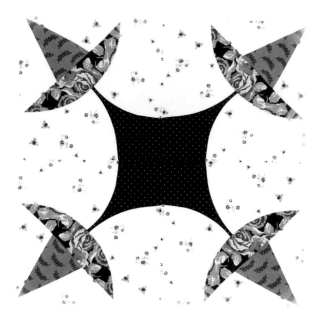
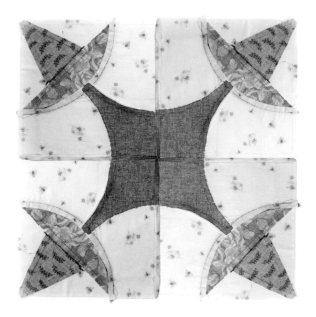

Cutting

From the LIGHT fabric, cut:

(4)   A pieces

(4)   A pieces reversed

(4)   D pieces

(4)   D pieces reversed

From the DARK fabric, cut:

(4)   B pieces

(4)   C pieces

(4)   E pieces

Stitching Techniques

Refer to page 20,
Straight Running Stitch

Refer to page 34,
Stitching Curves

Press seams in one direction.

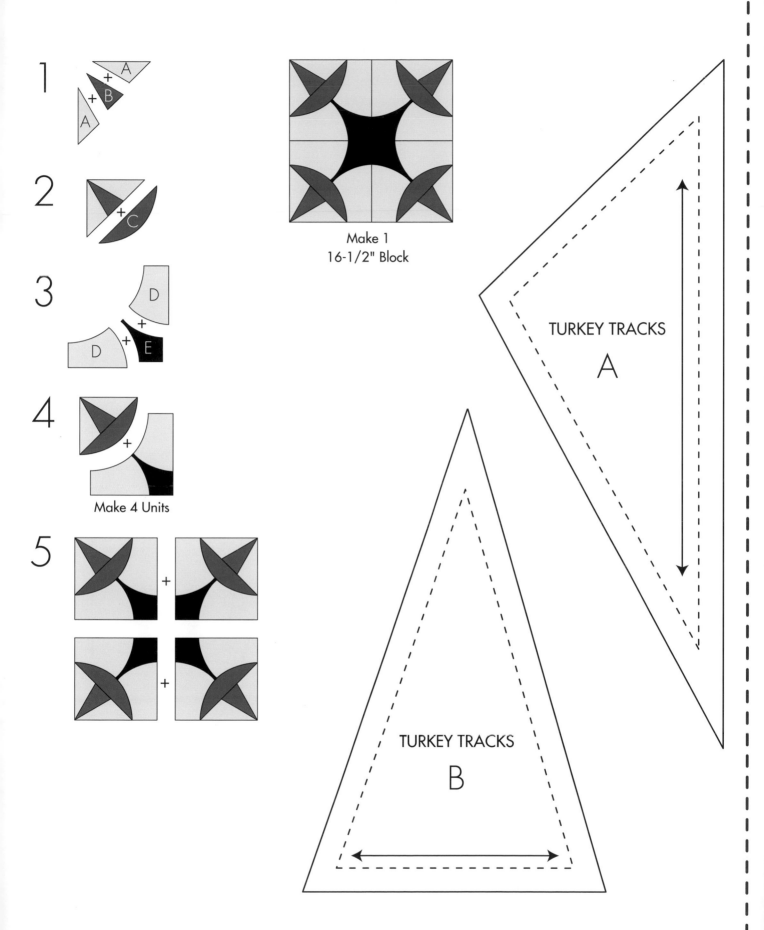

1

2

3

4

Make 4 Units

5

Make 1
16-1/2" Block

TURKEY TRACKS

A

TURKEY TRACKS

B

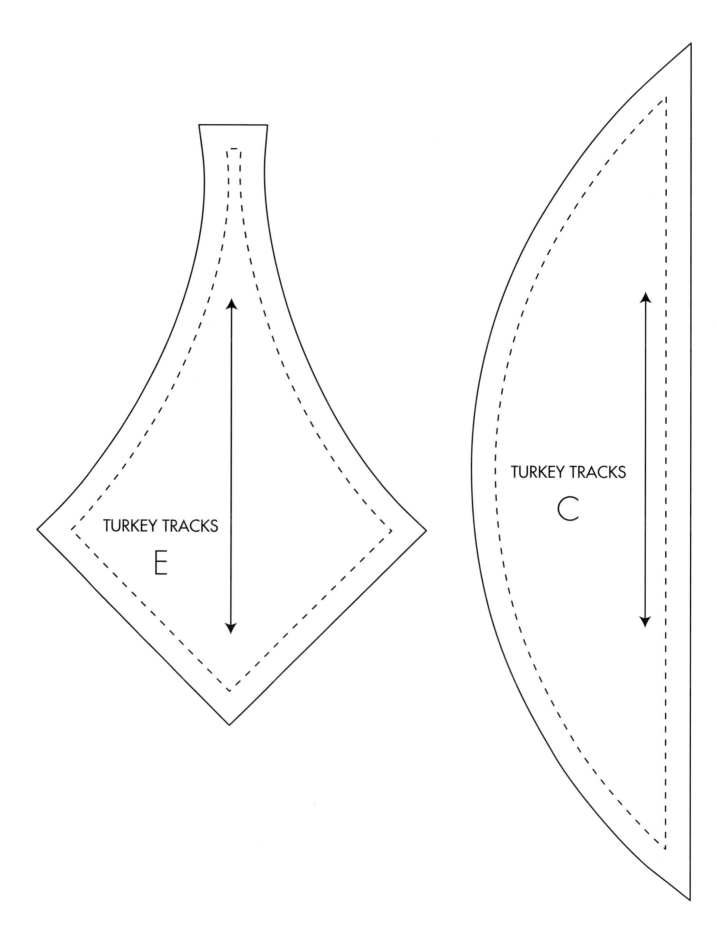

TURKEY TRACKS

E

TURKEY TRACKS

C

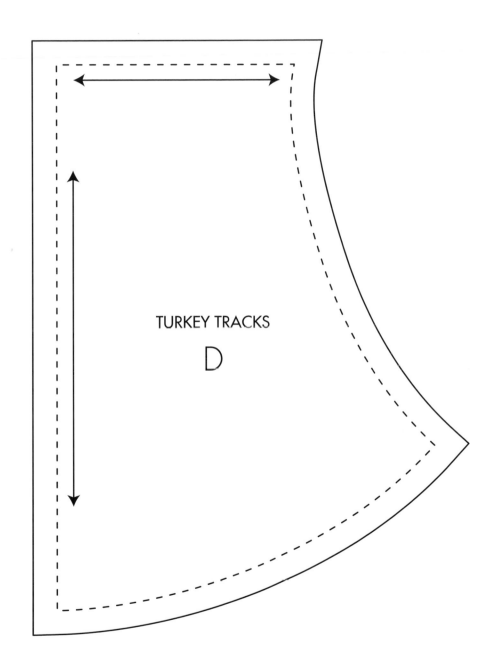

TURKEY TRACKS

D

Pieced Sunflower

Cutting

From the LIGHT fabric, cut:

(4)   A pieces

From the DARK fabric, cut:

(6)   B pieces

(1)   C piece

(6)   D pieces

Stitching Techniques

Refer to page 20,
Straight Running Stitch

Refer to page 30,
Stitching Set-In Seams

Refer to page 34,
Stitching Curves

Press seams as shown.

1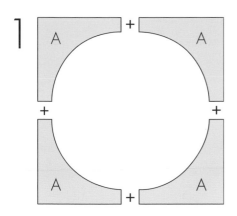

2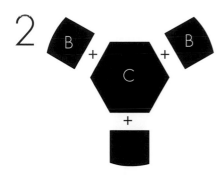

3
Make 3 Units

4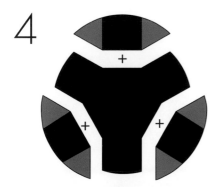

5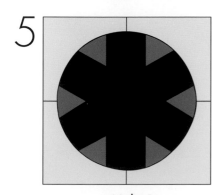
Make 1
12-1/2" Block

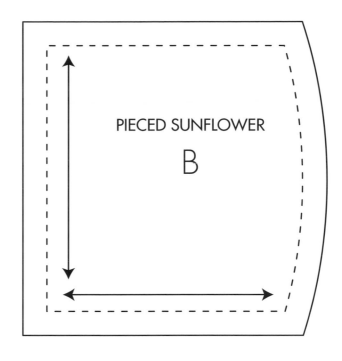

PIECED SUNFLOWER

B

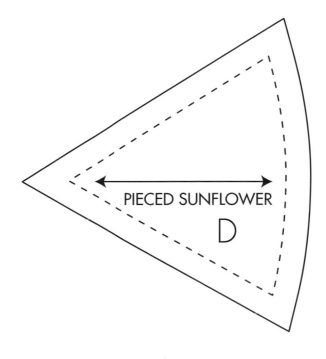

PIECED SUNFLOWER

D

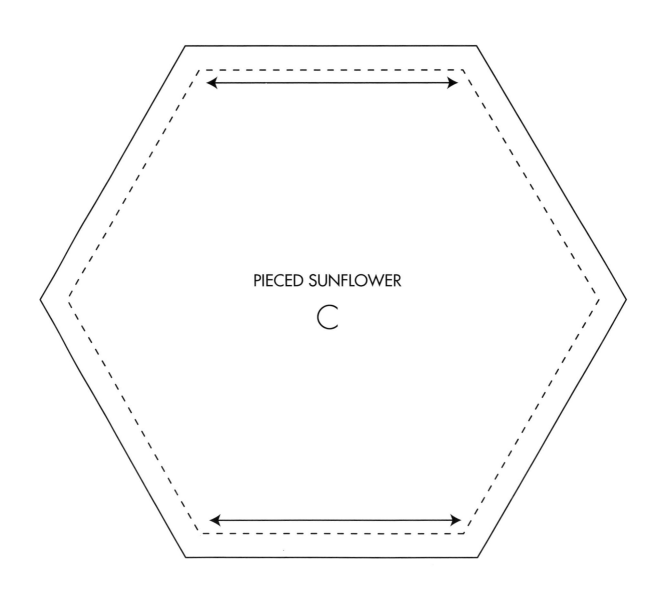

PIECED SUNFLOWER

C

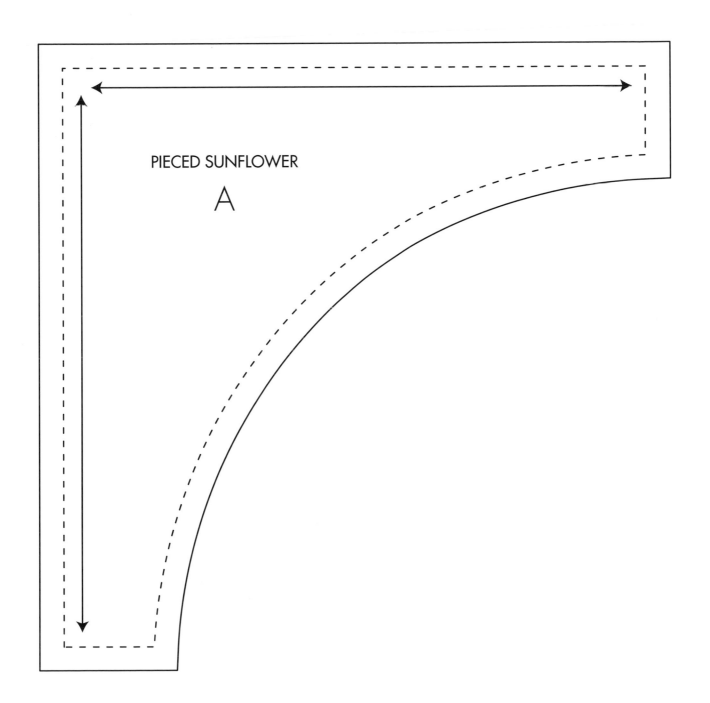

PIECED SUNFLOWER

A

Lily of the Valley

 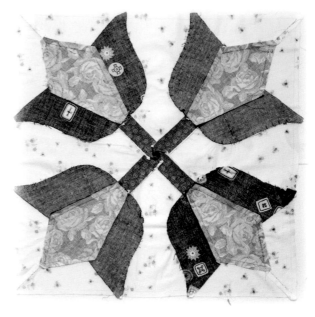

Cutting

From the LIGHT fabric, cut:

(4)   C pieces

(4)   C pieces reversed

(4)   D pieces

From the DARK fabric, cut:

(4)   A pieces

(4)   B pieces

(4)   B pieces reversed

(4)   E pieces

Stitching Techniques

Refer to page 20,
Straight Running Stitch

Refer to page 30,
Stitching Set-In Seams

Refer to page 34,
Stitching Curves

Press seams as shown.

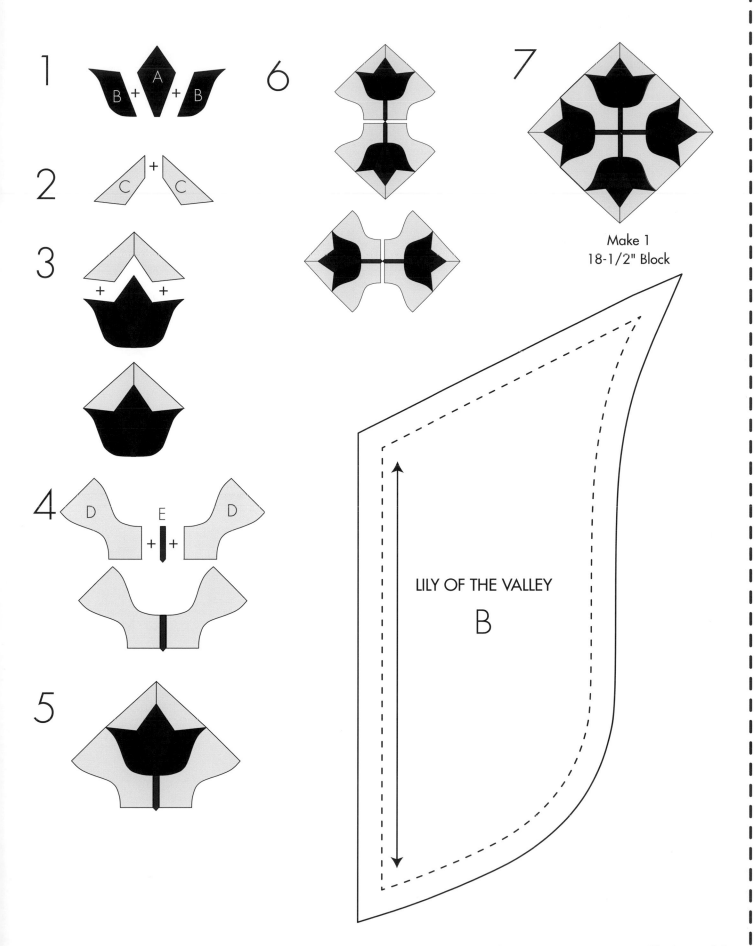

1

2

3

4

5

6

7

Make 1
18-1/2" Block

D E D

LILY OF THE VALLEY

B

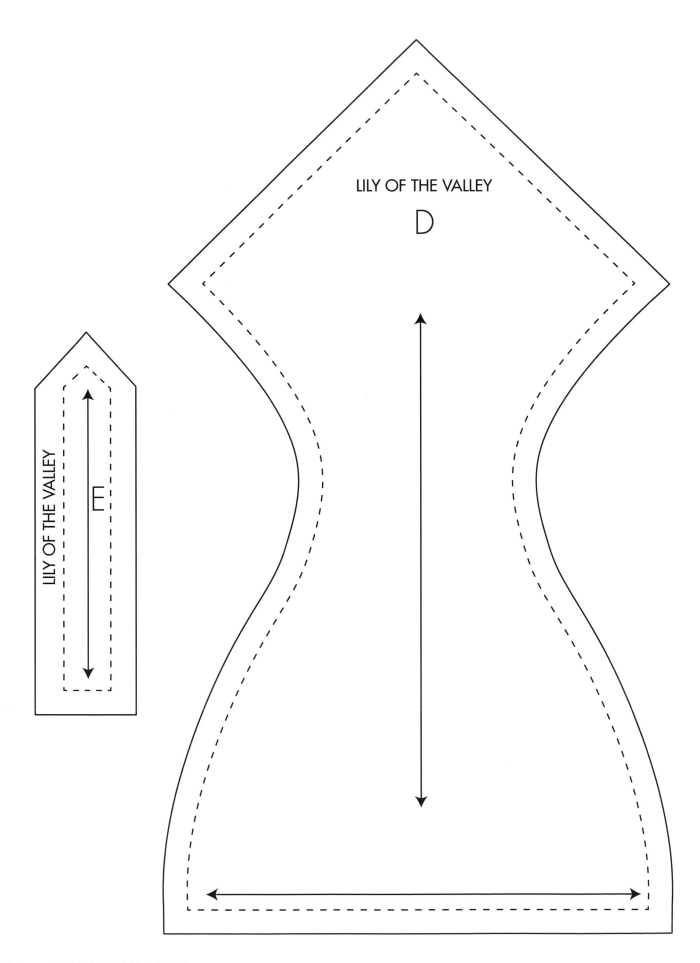

LILY OF THE VALLEY

D

LILY OF THE VALLEY

E

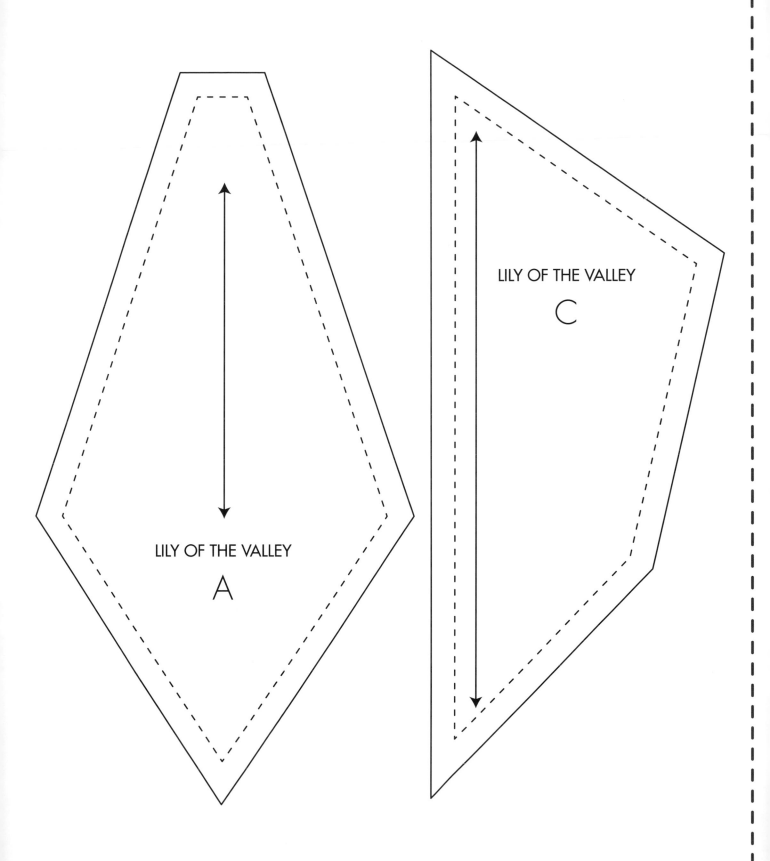

LILY OF THE VALLEY

A

LILY OF THE VALLEY

C

Caesar's Crown

From the LIGHT fabric, cut:

(4)   D pieces

(4)   E pieces

(4)   E pieces reversed

From the DARK fabric, cut:

(8)   A pieces

(8)   B pieces

(1)   C piece

Stitching Techniques

Refer to page 20,
Straight Running Stitch

Refer to page 30,
Stitching Set-In Seams

Refer to page 34,
Stitching Curves

Press seams as shown.

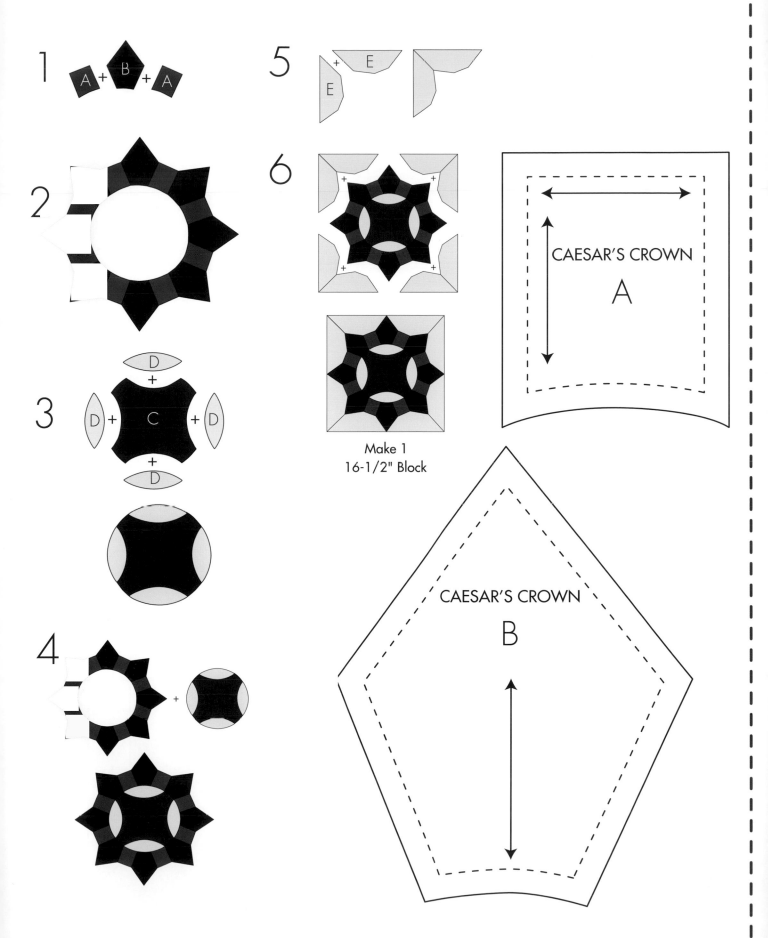

1 A + B + A

2

3 D
   +
   D + C + D
   +
   D

4 +

5 E + E

6 +   +

   +   +

   Make 1
   16-1/2" Block

CAESAR'S CROWN
A

CAESAR'S CROWN
B

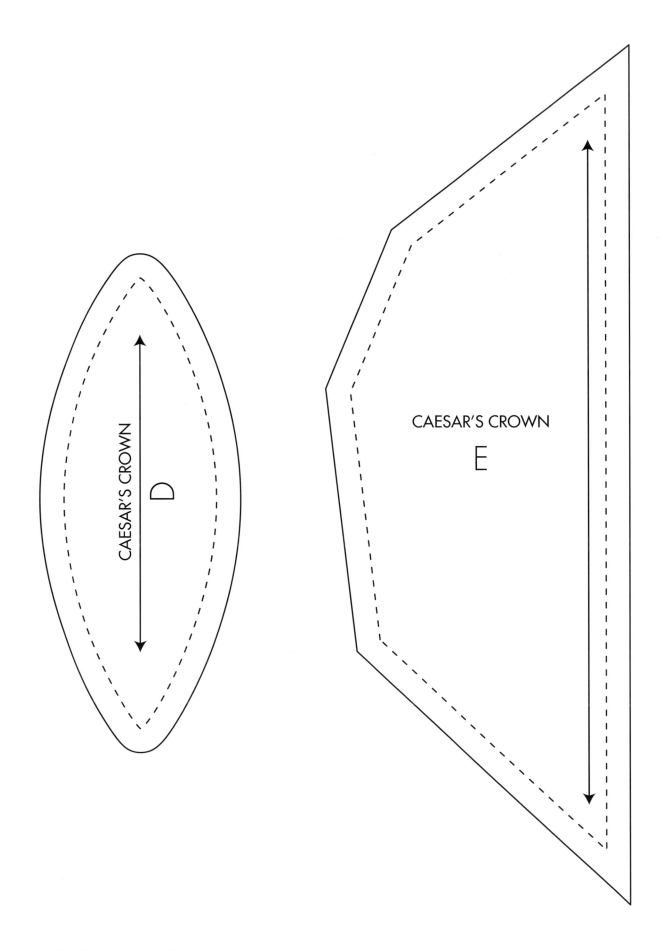

CAESAR'S CROWN

D

CAESAR'S CROWN

E

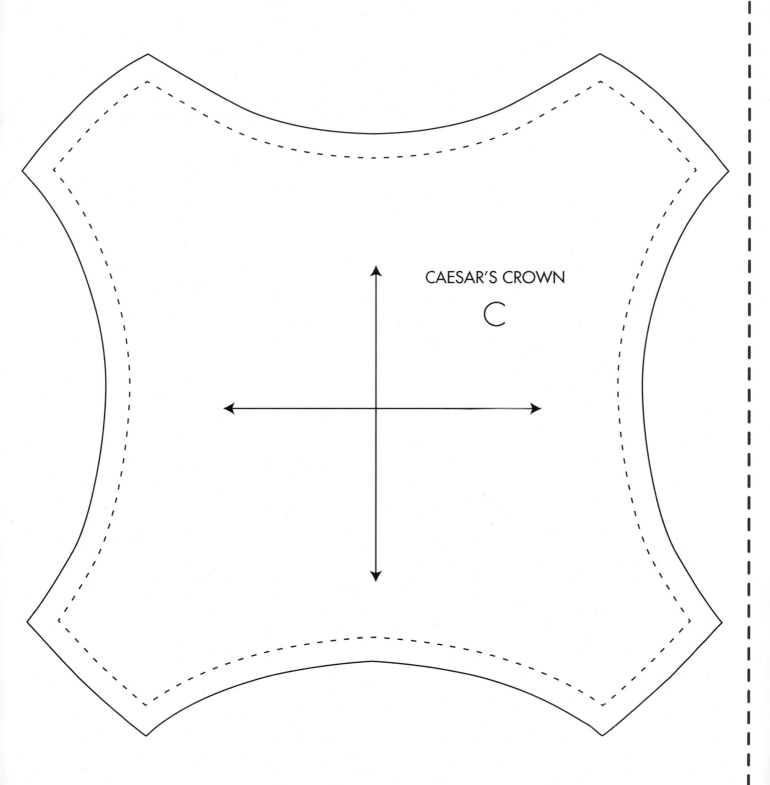

CAESAR'S CROWN

C

Hands All Around

Cutting

From the LIGHT fabric, cut:

(1) A piece

(4) E pieces

(4) C pieces

(4) F pieces

(8) G pieces

From the DARK fabric, cut:

(4) B pieces

(16) D pieces

Stitching Techniques

Refer to page 20,
Straight Running Stitch

Refer to page 30,
Stitching Set-In Seams

Refer to page 34,
Stitching Curves

Press seams as shown.

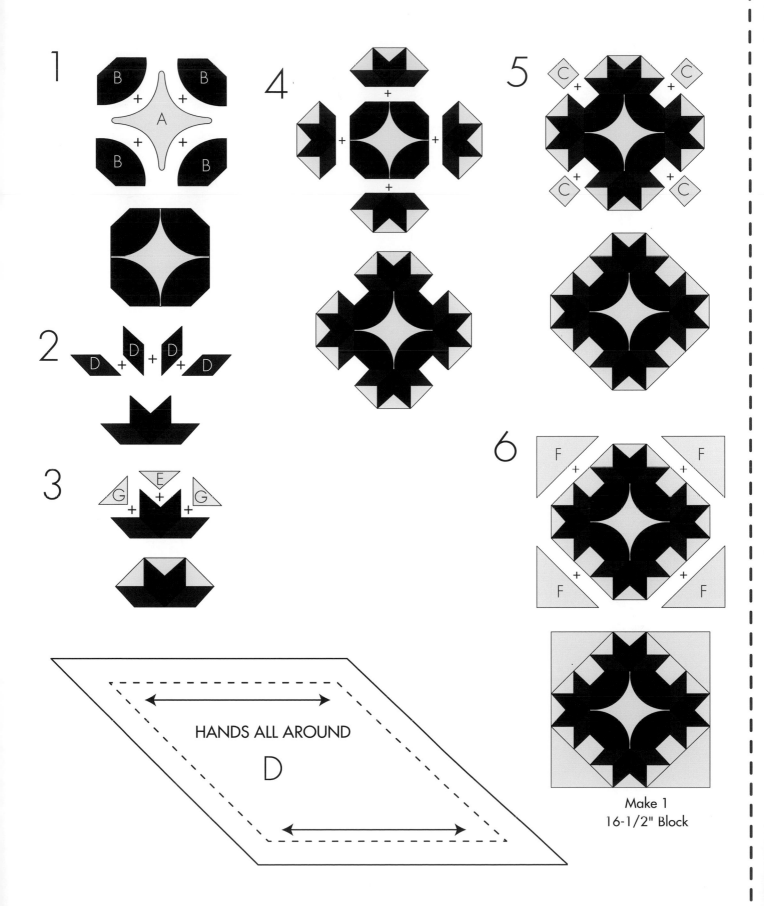

HANDS ALL AROUND

D

Make 1
16-1/2" Block

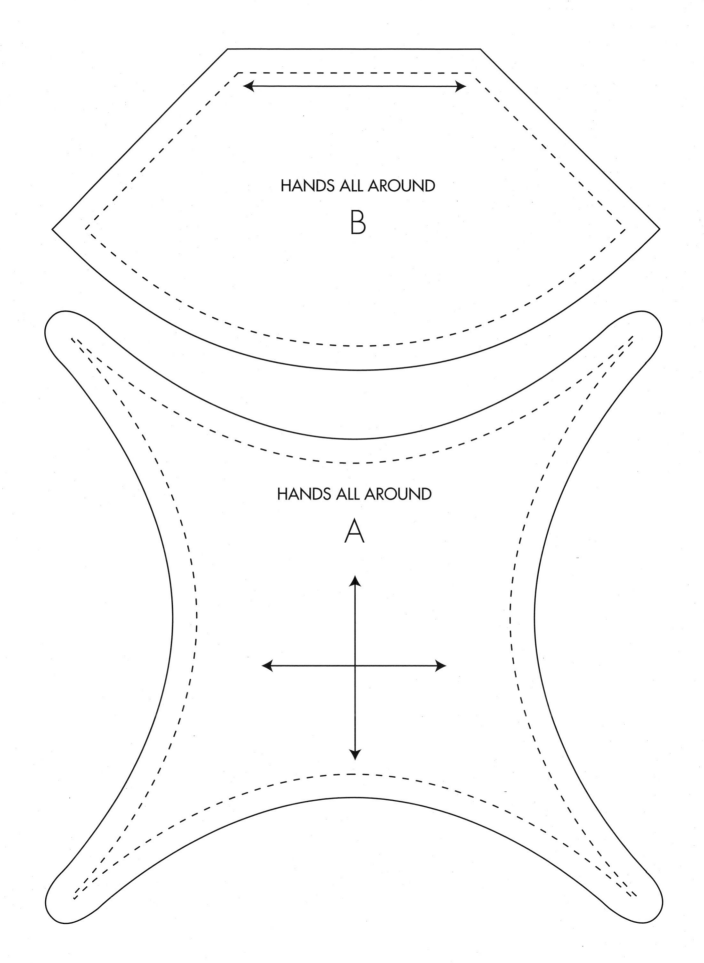

HANDS ALL AROUND

B

HANDS ALL AROUND

A

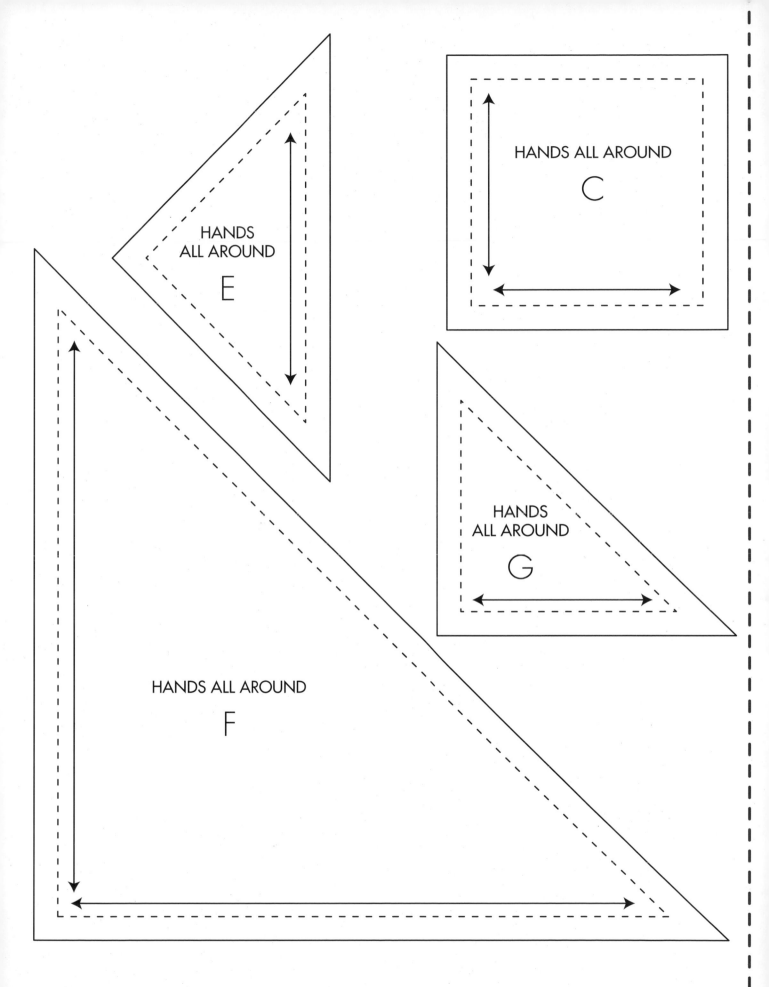

HANDS ALL AROUND
E

HANDS ALL AROUND
C

HANDS ALL AROUND
G

HANDS ALL AROUND
F

Making the Quilt

Now that your blocks are complete, you can start sewing them together in sections following the instructions on page 98. Lay the sections out following the diagram on page 101 to complete the quilt top.

Fabric Requirements

For the quilts in the book I used a scrappy combination of fabrics. You may wish to start with a themed group of fabrics to give you your direction and help make the choices easier along the way.

I suggest you start off with four or five fat quarters of fabrics that you like together and then as you sew your way through the blocks, introduce more fabrics as you work.

For the rest of the quilt, the information below will help with your fabric requirements.

Tip: Once your fabrics are cut, it's a good idea to keep the pieces for each block together. You can use small kitchen food bags, straight or safety pins, or project clips to hold the block pieces together.

Block Fabric:
- 1 Fat Quarter (18" x 22") for each block

Some may use all of it and some less.

Background Fabric:
- 4 yards (generous)

The color is up to you. You can match it with the border fabric or choose a pattern.

Border Fabric:
- 1-1/2 yards

Cut: (8) 6-1/2" x WOF strips

Backing Fabric:
- 4-1/2 yards

Cut into two equal lengths. Remove the selvedge and stitch together along the length with 3/8" seam. Press open.

- Batting: 86" x 88"

Binding:
- 5/8 yard

Cut: (8) 2-1/2" x WOF strips. Make a continuous strip with bias joins and press open. Press the entire length wrong sides together.

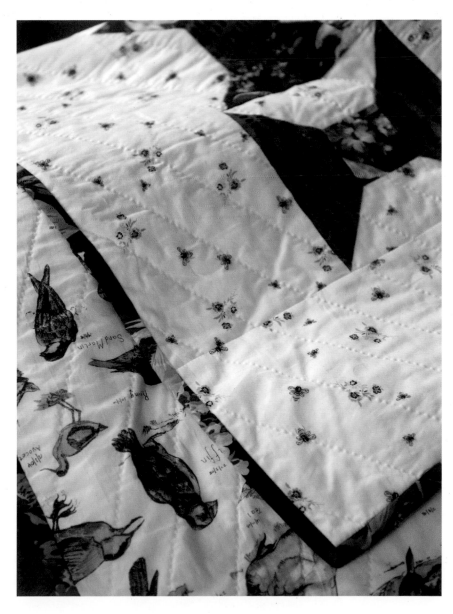

Stitching the Quilt Together

Following the diagrams, stitch the blocks into sections.

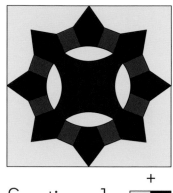

Section 1

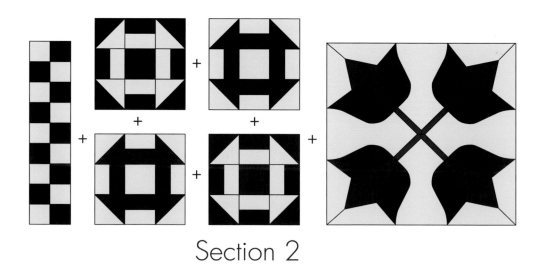

Section 2

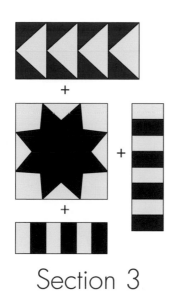

Section 3

Section 4

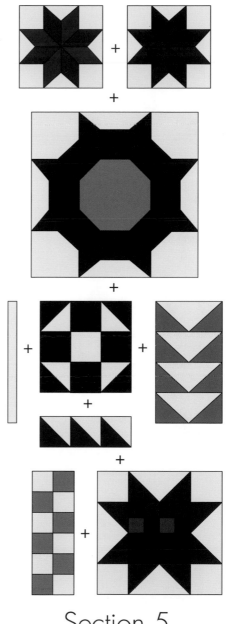

Section 5

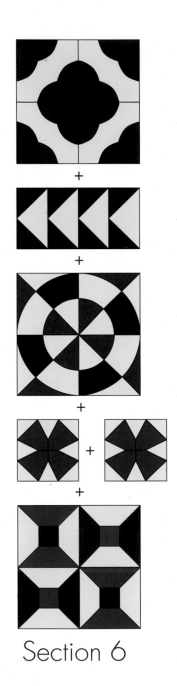

Section 6

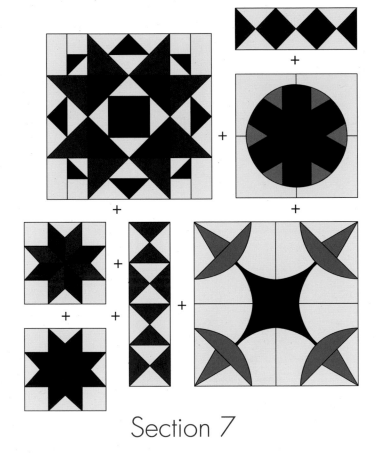

Section 7

Stitching the Sections Together

Once the sections are stitched together lay them out as shown and continue stitching the sections together to complete the quilt top.

Section 1

Section 2

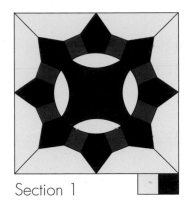

Section 3

Section 4

Section 5

Section 6

Section 7

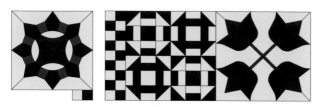

1 Stitch Section 1 and Section 2 together.

2 Next stitch Section 3 to the bottom left hand side.

3 Stitch Section 4. Gradually you will see that all of the pieces are coming together and as you sew by hand you can deal with setting and sewing around the corners.

4 Stitch Section 5.

5 Stitch Section 6 to the right hand side.

6 And lastly Section 7 to the left hand side. The top can be pressed and is now ready for the borders to be added.

color inspiration

Choose a beautiful array of pastel fabrics for a completely different look. See pages 142-143 for more ideas on color inspiration and the Amish Wave quilting option.

Making the Borders

From border fabric, cut:
(8) 6-1/2" x WOF strips

From the strips, cut:
Top Border
 (1) 6-1/2" x 16-1/2" piece
 (1) 6-1/2" x 42-1/2" piece

Bottom Border
 (1) 6-1/2" x 36-1/2" piece
 (1) 6-1/2" x 24-1/2" piece

Right Border
 (1) 6-1/2" x 30-1/2" piece
 (1) 6-1/2" x 12-1/2" piece
 (1) 6-1/2" x 18-1/2" piece

Left Border
 (1) 6-1/2" x 22-1/2" piece
 (1) 6-1/2" x 9-1/2" piece
 (1) 6-1/2" x 32-1/2" piece

1 For top border, sew the 6-patch unit to the right side of the 16-1/2" piece. Sew the 42-1/2' piece to the unit to complete the top border.

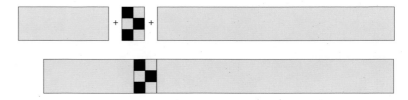

2 For bottom border, sew the 6-patch unit to the right side of the 36-1/2" piece. Sew the 24-1/2" piece to the unit to complete the bottom border.

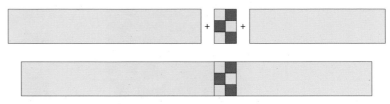

3 For left border, sew the Flying Geese unit to the right side of the 22-1/2" piece. Sew the 9-1/2" piece to the right side of the unit. Sew the Chinese Coin unit to the right side of the unit. Sew the 32-1/2" piece to the right side of the unit to complete the left border.

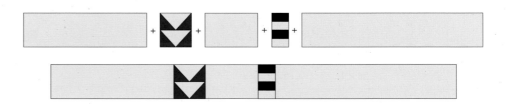

4 For right border, sew the Flying Geese unit to the right side of the 30-1/2" piece. Sew the 12-1/2" piece to the right side of the unit. Sew the Mayflower unit to the right side of the unit. Sew the 18-1/2" piece to the right side of the unit to complete the right border.

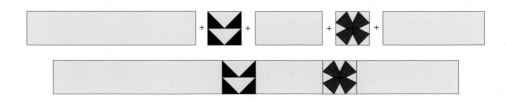

Stitching the Borders to the Quilt Center

The borders of the quilt "pinwheel" or "wrap" around the quilt center. Usually, this requires using the "partial seams" technique. But the following step-by-step eliminates the need to go back and pin partially sewn seams.

1 Layout the borders as shown.

2 Starting with the bottom border, align the pieced unit of the border with the matching unit in the quilt center. Stitch until you are 6" from the left border.

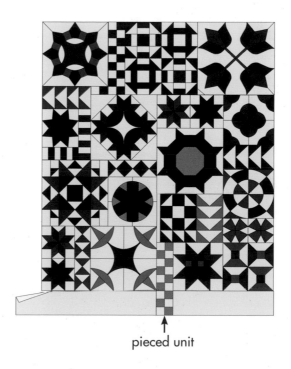

pieced unit

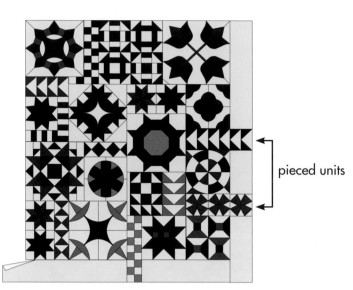

pieced unit

pieced units

3 Stitch the right border, aligning the pieced units with the matching units in the quilt center. Stitch the length of the border.

4 Stitch the top border, aligning the pieced unit with the matching unit in the quilt center. Stitch the length of the border.

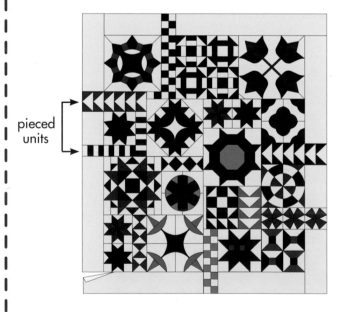

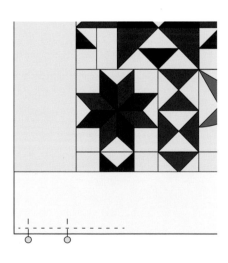

pieced units

5 Stitch the left border, aligning the pieced units with the matching units in the quilt center. Stitch the length of the border.

6 Fold the bottom border, RST, along the seam and pin. Stitch the unfinished seam to complete the border.

Making the Quilt Your Own

On the previous pages, you stitched the quilt blocks together in sections to make the quilt the same as mine. But you might consider swapping blocks or sections to give the quilt your own personality. On page 108, the diagram gives you measurements for each finished block.
Page 109 gives you an option to change the look of your quilt simply by changing the direction of sections.

The chart below gives you some options on how to substitute blocks. Try changing out larger blocks for multiples of smaller ones.

6" Blocks

Mayflower   Spools

Substitute:

Two Flying Geese (3" x 6")   Four Half-Square Triangles (3")

8" Blocks

Le Moyne Star

Substitute:

4" Quarter-Square Triangle Blocks

9" Blocks

Churn Dash   Amish Star

12" Blocks

Signature Block   16-Patch Sawtooth Star

Substitute:
6" Blocks, see page 108

16" Blocks

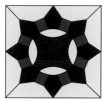 
Caeser's Crown   Hands all Around

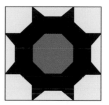 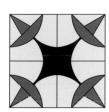
Castle Wall   Turkey Tracks

Substitute:
8" blocks, see page 108
4" blocks, see page 108

18" Blocks

Lily of the Valley Block

Substitute:
9" blocks, see page 108
6" blocks, see page 108

Block Size Placement

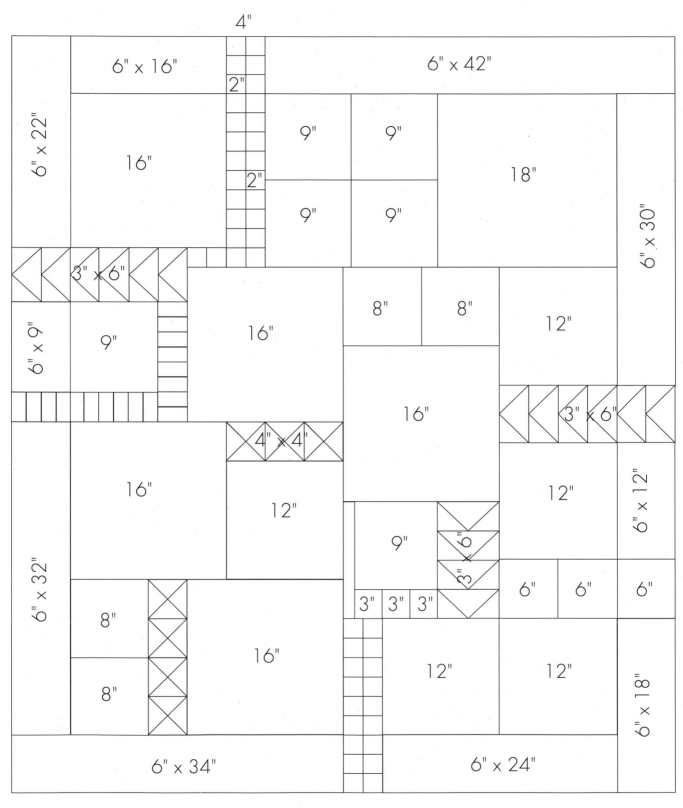

Switching Sections Around

Another idea to make the quilt your own would be to simply turn sections around. Section 2, 6 and 7 would be good candidates for this.

Section 2, page 98

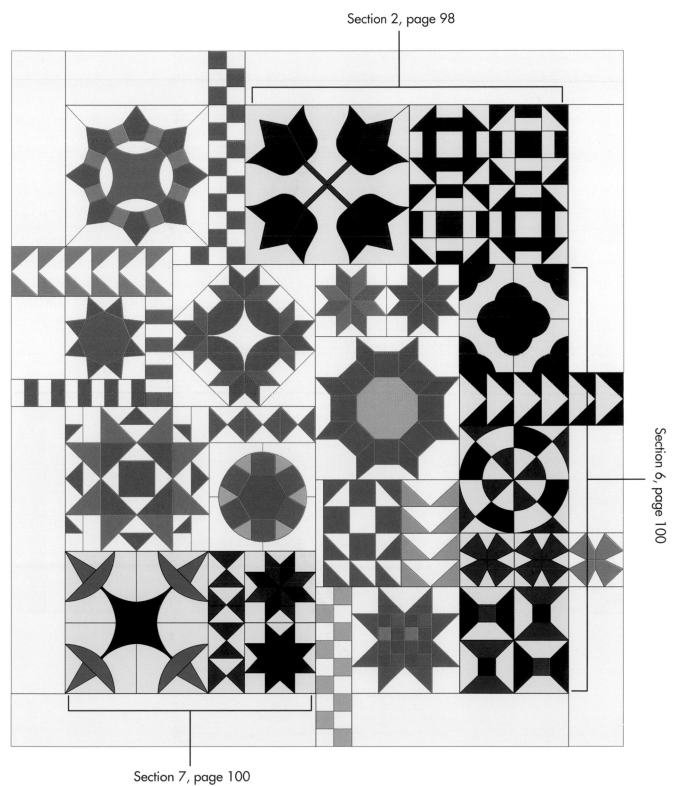

Section 6, page 100

Section 7, page 100

Layering and Basting the Quilt

Once you have sewn your patchwork top, it's ready to layer with batting and backing fabric and then ready to quilt.

Backing fabric

Yardage listed for the background fabric is generous. It needs to be wider and longer than the quilt top. As you quilt, the top and batting will shrink or pull up. Surplus fabric and batting will be trimmed when you are ready to bind the quilt. **Note:** Wide width fabrics are available for backing and these will eliminate seams on the back of your quilt.

Choose a fabric that is similar in weight to the fabric you used in your blocks. Since you are hand quilting you will want a fabric that will be as easy to work with as the fabrics in your blocks. The fabric can be plain or patterned but remember if you choose a plain color, your quilting stitches will be highly visible. Patterned fabric tends to hide stitches.

If you choose fabric that needs joining, follow these basic tips. First, remove the selvedges from the fabric. Sew a 3/8" seam and press open to reduce bulk where you may need to quilt through. Seams can be horizontal, vertical, or pieced so that the second width of fabric is sewn to either side of the full width. This method works well if you are concerned about the stress that is caused from folding your quilt in half on the seam line.

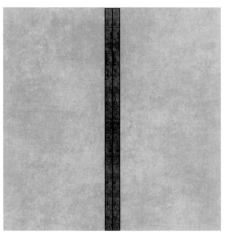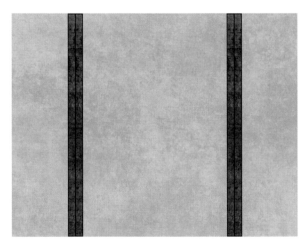

Batting

In the U.K. where I live, batting is referred to as "wadding". It's the puffy bit that goes between the quilt top and backing fabric. It can be made from cotton, wool, polyester, bamboo, even plastic bottles. Most important when choosing batting is how much quilting you want and how "puffy" you want your quilt. The puffiness is known as "loft" and will give your quilt its characteristic look.

On batting packaging, information will be available to tell you fiber content, dimensions, approximate loft, shrinkage (if any) and most importantly maximum distance between stitches. Depending on the batting, it may be as much as 10" apart or as little as 2"-4" apart. Remember that the quilting holds the layers together so it's important to use the appropriate loft to accomplish the look you want on your finished quilt.

Quilting Thread

The thread you choose for quilting should be slightly thicker than general sewing thread. It will form the stitches that hold the three layers of your quilt together. When shopping for quilting thread, look for spools that say "quilting thread".

Choose a color that blends with the overall appearance of the quilt. If you want the stitches to stand out, choose a color with more contrast.

If you choose to hand quilt with Big Stitch Quilting, pages 126-131, you can us a thicker cotton thread like 8 or 12 Cotton Perle, or Aurifil 12.

Quilting Needles

Quilting needles are usually short with a round eye. Betweens or Quilting needles are a good choice. They come in a range of sizes to accommodate thread and skill level. Beginners often start with size 8, which is a bigger needle, and then work towards a 10 or 11, which are smaller needles. The smaller the needle the smaller your stitch will be. Sometimes it comes down to practicing and sometimes, the combination of the fabric and batting.

If you choose to quilt with big stitches and use a thicker thread, try Betweens size 6 or an Embroidery needle size 6. They are bigger needles with bigger eyes to accommodate the thicker thread.

Basting

Hand basting a quilt gives you the best control over the layers and does not add any extra weight or bulk.

General Equipment

Basting Thread

Needles

Grapefruit spoon

Safety pins

Kwik Klip™

Masking tape

Kneeling pads or mat

Generally for all methods of basting, the securing method should form a grid, often dictated by the patches in the quilt. There should not be a gap bigger than 6" between the basting, about the size of your spread hand. If the patchwork does not have a grid to follow, use your hand span as the ready guide.

How to Hand Baste

Use specialist tacking thread as this breaks easily and is cheaper that regular sewing thread.

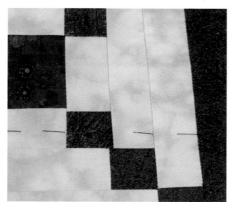

1 When hand basting a quilt, start with a knot and a backstitch.

2 The stitches will be about a 1/2" long and evenly spaced. Remember to form a grid while tacking. Refer to page XX, Systems to Baste the Layers together.

TIPS FOR HAND BASTING

- Use a flat floor that is already clean where the quilt will lay out flat. Community and church halls have this space, but be sure to reserve it when you know it's just been cleaned. Another option is using their large tables if kneeling on the floor is a problem. Using these spaces will save you from having to move your own furniture around to make room for a quilt on the floor.

- For any basting done on the floor consider using a kneeling mat or knee pads to protect your knees during the process.

- If using a carpeted floor this will stop the quilt from moving so much and the edges can be secured with masking tape.

- Use the services of a long arm quilter. Many offer a basting service, making it easier and faster for you to sit down and enjoy the quilting.

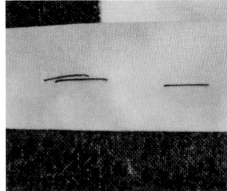

4 Finish with a backstitch to keep the thread secure.

3 To help ease the needle up through the layers use a teaspoon or grapefruit spoon. Since the needle and your hands are always on the top of the quilt, your fingers can get sore as the needle pushes up against them. Pushing the needle up against the edge of a grapefruit spoon makes the process quicker.

Assembling the Quilt Layers for Basting

The three layers of your quilt–backing, batting and top–need to be smooth and free of wrinkles before the basting process can be done. Basting will keep the layers securely together for quilting.

Press the backing fabric and lay it on the floor wrong side up. Smooth it out flat, securing it to the floor with masking tape at the corners and mid-points on all four sides.

Note: DO NOT stretch the fabric. If you stretch the fabric, it will retract back to its natural place when the masking tape comes off after basting. This will cause puckers in your quilt back.

Fold the batting into quarters. Line up the outside edge of the batting with the corner of the backing fabric and unfold a quarter at a time, smoothing the batting over the backing fabric. The middle of the backing and batting should now be centered.

Press the quilt top and place it on top of the batting, right side up. You may also fold the quilt top into quarters, as was done with the batting. Leave approximately 2-1/2" of batting showing around the edge of the quilt top.

Smooth out the quilt top until it is flat and free of wrinkles. Add squares of masking tape at the corners.

Safety pin the three layers together in the center, at the corners and at the mid-point of each side. This keeps things in place while basting.

Basting the layers together

When basting a quilt I find it easier to baste in a grid system.

If I always use the same system, then I don't have to think or plan, just baste! I baste the quilts on a carpeted floor. This helps keep the layers from shifting.

Tip

If you have hardwood or linoleum floors, they may need protection from the needle. Protect the floor by using a rotary cutting mat between the backing and the floor and move the mat as you baste. You can also tabletop baste your quilts.

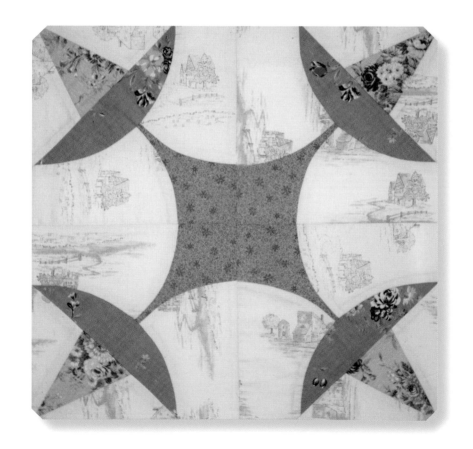

Grid Systems for Basting your Quilt

When basting a quilt, I find it easier to keep a grid system as I baste. There are several ways to form a grid on your quilt. Read through the systems and choose the one that will work best for you.

System One

This is the system I use when I hand baste my quilts on the floor. It smooths out any wrinkles that may arise.

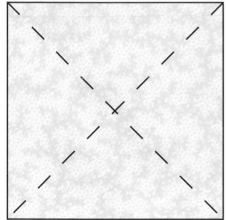
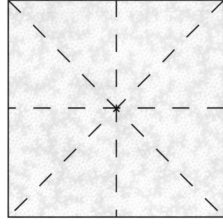
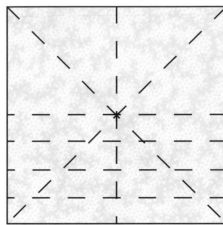

1 Using basting thread, begin with a knot and a backstitch. Begin basting the diagonal lines. For ease, use a teaspoon or grapefruit spoon (see page 113) to bring the needle up and out of the quilt. Since you are working from the top at all times, there is no need to have a hand under the quilt. This would disturb the layers.

2 Baste across the middle in both directions. Take out pins as you come to them.

3 Using your hand span as a guide, baste in rows beginning in the center and working toward the outer edge. When this section is full, move to the next.

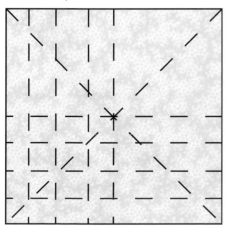
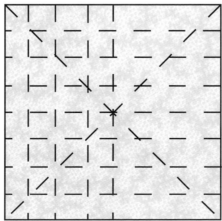
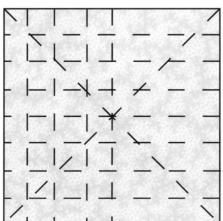

4 Baste all four sections in the same manner as Step 3. Remember to always start your line of basting in the quilt center and work toward the outer edge.

5 When the grid is complete, baste 1/4" from the outside edge of the quilt layers. This will stop the edges from fraying or stretching before quilting, The stitches will be removed as you quilt. Remove the masking tape from the edges of your quilt layers. You can now fold the extra batting and backing fabric over and baste it, abutting it with the edge of the quilt top.

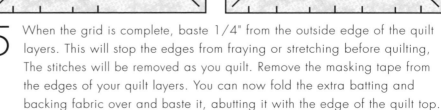

System Two
This system allows the quilt to be evenly basted in smaller sections.

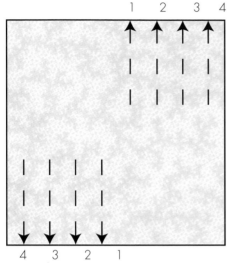

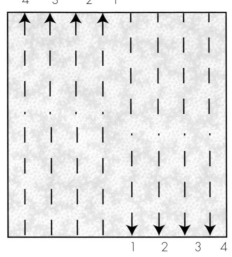

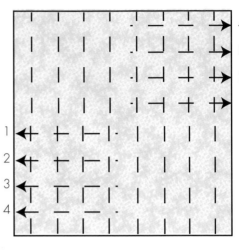

1 Baste the first two sections in vertical rows as shown, beginning in the center and working toward the outer edge. Take out pins as you come to them.

2 Continue with the next two sections.

3 Return to the first two sections and baste in horizontal rows as shown.

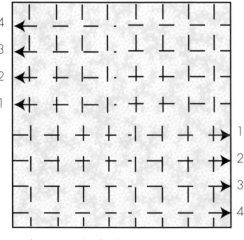

4 Baste the final two sections in horizontal rows.

When the grid is complete, baste 1/4" from the outside edge of the quilt layers. This will stop the edges from fraying or stretching before quilting. The stitches will be removed as you quilt.

Remove the masking tape from the edges of your quilt layers. You can now fold the extra batting and backing fabric over and tack it, abutting it with the edge of the quilt top.

System Three

This system works from the center outward like the rays of the sun. It has the appearance of a radial, less rigid grid.

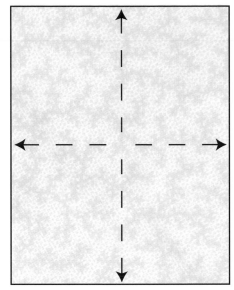

1 Baste the center lines, beginning in the middle of the quilt layers and working toward the outer edge. Take out pins as you come to them.

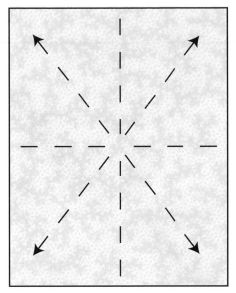

2 Baste diagonal lines between the center lines, as shown.

3 Continue basting diagonal lines in the same manner until the quilt layers are secure.

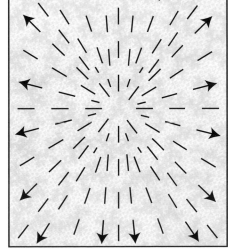

When the grid is complete, baste 1/4" from the outside edge of the quilt layers. This will stop the edges from fraying or stretching before quilting. The stitches will be removed as you quilt.

Remove the masking tape from the edges of your quilt layers. You can now fold the extra batting and backing fabric over and tack it, abutting it with the edge of the quilt top.

Tabletop Basting

If you are unable to baste or hand tack your quilt on the floor, try tabletop basting. You can baste a large quilt on a table using clips or clamps to hold it in place.

Things You Will Need for Tabletop Basting

- A table at a comfortable height for you
  Note: If the table is not high enough, invest in plastic piping that will fit on the bottom of the legs, increasing the height, or purchase table risers.
- An adjustable office chair so you can sit to baste
- Masking tape, toothpicks or skewers
- Clips, clamps or Bulldog clips
- Sharps size 6 needle or needle of your choice (if hand basting)
- Basting or other thread (if hand basting)
- Safety pins (if pin basting)

1 Mark the center of the table, vertically and horizontally, with a toothpick, skewer or other thin object. Keep in place with masking tape.

Note: I do this so I can feel the center of the table through the quilt layers. You may also place masking tape at the mid-point of each side of the table.

2 Press the backing fabric and fold into quarters, wrong sides together.

Place the folded backing fabric on the table, matching the center of the fabric with the center of the table.

3 Unfold the fabric with wrong side up. Line up the edges with the sides of the table to keep it straight. Use clips to secure the fabric to the edges of the table.

Note: If the quilt is smaller than the table, tape the edges down on the table top.

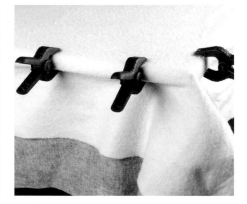

4 Fold the batting in the same way and place it on top of the backing fabric matching the center points. Smooth the batting over the backing fabric. Do not stretch it. Clip into place using the same clips used for the backing.

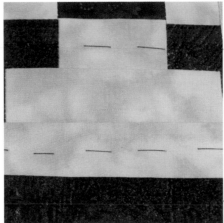

5 Press the quilt top and fold into quarters, right sides together. Place the quilt top on the batting matching the center points. Smooth out any creases as you unfold the quilt top. Use the clips to hold the three layers together.

6 Baste the area secured on the table. Baste in rows approximately 6" apart.

7 If the quilt top and layers are hanging off your table, remove the clips when the first area is complete. Shift the layers away from you so the next unbasted area is on the tabletop. Secure the side of the quilt that has been basted with clips or masking tape. Pull the backing taut and secure the next unbasted section with clips to the opposite side of the tabletop. Baste as before.

Continue this process until the entire quilt has been basted. You may need to move the quilt several times to completely baste it.

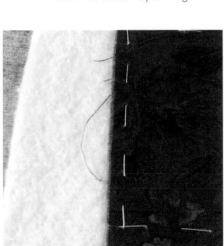

8 When finished, baste 1/4" around the outside edge of the quilt top.

Other Tacking and Basting Options

If hand basting a quilt comfortably and quickly is not an option for you, consider one of the alternative techniques listed here. For maximum efficiency, combine any of the following techniques with tabletop basting.

Tools to Make it Quicker

1" safety pins (open)

Safety pin covers

Kwik Klip™ or grapefruit spoon

Safety Pin Basting

When basting with safety pins, they should be placed approximately every 6" to 8". Test this with the span of your hand. If your hand is spread out on the quilt top and you are not touching safety pins, add a few more.

Use a Kwik Klip™ or grapefruit spoon to close the safety pins. Plastic covers are also available for safety pins giving your fingers something larger to grip. All three of these tools will help you avoid sore fingers.

Layer the backing, batting and quilt top following steps 1–5 in Tabletop Basting on pages 118-119.

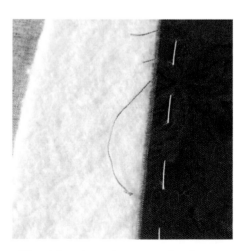

1 Beginning at the center and working from the top of the quilt, insert the safety pin and bring it back up through all three layers. Bring the point of the safety pin up against the edge of the grapefruit spoon or Kwik Klip™ and clip it closed.

2 Continue to pin baste the quilt layers. Do a hand span check every once in a while to make sure you are spacing the safety pins correctly. The pins should not be too densely or sparsely placed. If you can spread your hand on the quilt and touch pins, that is a good density.

3 When the quilt is covered with pins, baste 1/4" around the outside edge of the quilt top.

Spray Adhesives

Quilt layers may also be held together with spray adhesives, such as 505 Spray and Fix or Sulky® Temporary Spray Adhesive. It is odorless and will hold the layers together while you quilt. Follow the product instructions and work on the quilt in sections.

Tacking or Basting Gun

A tacking or basting gun is a quick way to baste your quilt layers before quilting. This tool resembles the gun that attaches price tags to clothing. I recommend testing on scraps of leftover fabric before using on your quilt layers. Be sure to follow manufacturer's instructions carefully if you choose this method of basting.

When preparing your quilt layers for stitching, consider the design you will be using. The quilt above was machine stitched in a straight grid. The quilt at left was hand quilted with a wave quilting design.

Quilting

This is quite simply a running stitch that will hold the three layers of your quilt sandwich together. Since you have been hand piecing you will find the process of quilting easy to get the hang of since the action is very similar, just more layers to stitch through.

Fine Hand Quilting

Fine hand quilting is the traditional form of stitching that will hold three layers of your quilt sandwich together. You might want to practice with a small quilt sandwich to become more comfortable with stitching through layers. Be sure to read through "Big Stitch Quilting" on pages 126-137, as an alternative to fine hand quilting.

Quilting Needles

Try Betweens in sizes 8-11. You might want to start using a larger needle like a size 8. (**Note:** the smaller the needle size, the larger the needle.) As you continue to stitch, you might want to try a smaller needle like a size 11. Your stitching motion will be slightly different with a smaller needle and it may be harder to thread. Look for a smaller needle with a larger eye.

Quilting Thread

Hand quilting thread is usually sold on spools marked as "Quilting Thread" and it will be a 40 wt, which is the thickness of the thread. I like to quilt with 28 wt. It's worth trying out some threads to see which you prefer since threads from different manufacturers may vary.

Thimbles and Finger Protection

If you have become accustomed to using a thimble, it is worth your while to continue using it. Pushing a needle through all the layers of your quilt requires extra force and using some form of finger protection will make the process easier. (See page 8 for thimble ideas.)

Quilting Hoops

Using a hoop will act like a third hand for you. The hoop frame holds the quilt allowing your two hands to work on stitches from underneath and on top of your work. If you have not used one before, there a few pointers to make things easier.

A 14" diameter wooden hoop is about 1" deep. This size works well for most people. Don't try an embroidery hoop; they are too shallow and your work is likely to pop out of the frame.

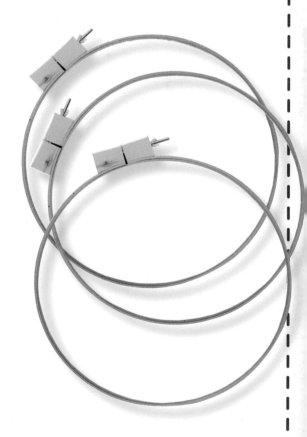

When you put your quilt in the hoop tighten it firmly to hold the quilt with no pleats around the edge. Make sure there is movement in the quilt by poking your finger up from underneath, making a "hill". You want to see an indentation of your fingernail. Tightening your quilt too much inside the hoop will make it harder to stitch and it will stretch your quilt.

Starting the Stitch

Just as you did when you started stitching the blocks, cut the length of the thread the length of your arm (page 19). This may seem short to some people but it will make the act of quilting easier since you will be pulling the thread through the fabric at the same pace and tension each time. Use this technique for fine hand and big stitch quilting.

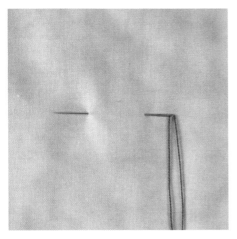 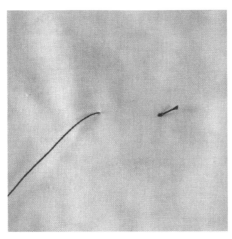 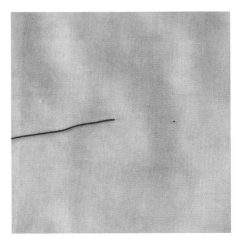

1 For the first stitch, cut and knot your thread as before. Insert the needle through the top layer of the quilt and batting, coming up to where you want your first stitch to start.

2 The knot should now be laying on the top layer of fabric.

3 To embed the knot in the batting, gently pull the thread until the knot 'pops' down into the batting. The embedded thread will be quilted over with your chosen stitch. This adds an extra layer of security for the thread.

Tip
If the knot is stubborn and won't pull through the fabric, use the point of the needle and push the weave of the fabric apart to expand the hole where the knot needs to go through. Gently pull the thread until the knot goes into the batting. Use the needle to push the threads back in place.

Ending the Stitch

When you are finished stitching or the thread is running out, you will need to secure your ending stitches. Leave approximately 5" – 6" of thread to end your stitch.

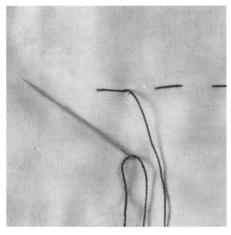

1 To secure the last stitch, go all the way through to the back of the quilt with the needle. Bring the needle up at the beginning of the last stitch.

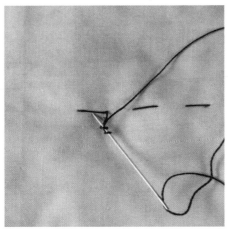

2 Pull the thread through and wrap it around the needle three times, keeping the thread close to the quilt.

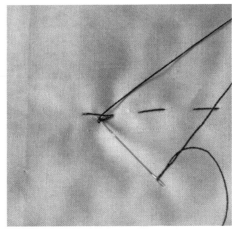

3 Push the needle into the middle of the last stitch, just underneath it and through the top layer and batting.

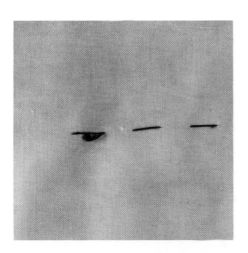

1 Travel approximately a needle's length away from the stitching, and bring the needle back up to the surface. As you pull the thread a knot will form.

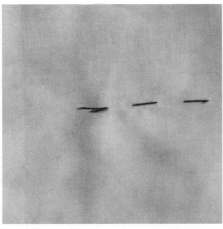

2 Gently pull the knot through to embed it in the batting. Snip the thread close to the quilt top.

Big Stitch Quilting

Big stitch quilting is a bolder style of quilting. The designs are usually more widely spaced, therefore needing fewer lines and less time to quilt. It also uses a thicker thread and longer stitches. The stitch length is often longer on the top layer of the quilt and smaller on the bottom layer. This style of stitching gives the quilt a chunkier, primitive, more masculine feel. It is sometimes referred to as Depression Stitching or Naïve Quilting.

Heavier Fabrics, Bigger Stitches

Many of the quilts we see from our ancestors or in museums were pieced from heavy wool fabrics. Therefore, the bigger stitches and thicker threads were needed, since fine thread and small stitches would not have held the layers together.

In some depression era (1930's) quilts the thick quilting thread was believed to be the sewing thread used to hold flour sacks together before they were cut and sewn into quilts. Using the bigger quilting stitch was another way to get the job done faster, when a flour sack quilt was one of the only affordable ways to keep warm at night.

A variety of stitches are shown on the following pages. Choose the ones that will enhance your quilt top and consider these tips while stitching.

Big Stitch Tips

- There are no rules when it comes to the number of utility stitches per inch, but as a general guideline try four to five stitches per inch. If you are using thicker threads the stitches can be bigger.

- As you stitch, try to keep a rhythm of creating large, even stitches that go through all three layers.

- Some people keep the needle hand still and move the finger on the underside of the quilt to create the stitches. Others do the exact opposite. Try different motions to find what is comfortable and creates the even stitches you want.

- I find it helpful to have a thimble on the middle finger of my needle hand for pushing the needle through and a ridged thimble on the index finger of my hand under the quilt.

- The finger under the quilt pushes the layers up creating a little hill with the ridge of the thimble. The needle is pushed against it to make the stitch.

- When there is approximately 6" of thread left in the needle, end your stitch and start a new length of thread.

Methodist Knot Stitch

The Methodist Knot stitch adds texture as it holds the three layers of the quilt together. The stitches work up quickly and you can develop a nice stitching rhythm.

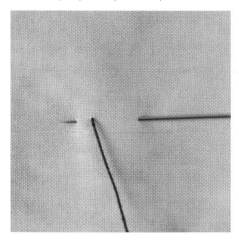

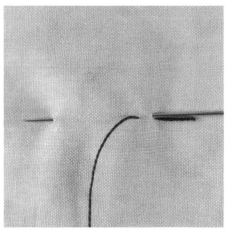

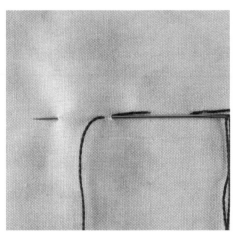

1 Review Starting the Stitch on page 124 to thread the needle and embed the knot in the batting along the line you will be stitching over. Come up through the top layer, bury the knot, and insert the needle down through all three layers. Bring the needle back up about one third length of the backstitch in front of it.

2 Push the needle down into the batting, creating a small backstitch. Travel the needle along to the next stitch.

3 Continue stitching in this way. End the stitch on the small backstitch, referring to Ending the Stitch on page 125.

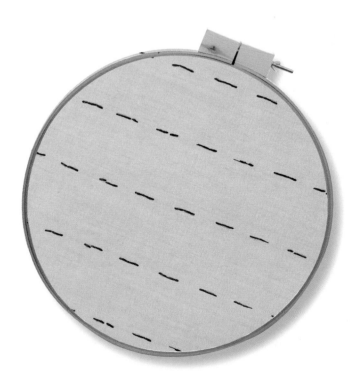

Modified Backstitch

The Modified Backstitch is worked in the same way as the Methodist Knot Stitch. However, the Modified Backstitch gives you a slightly bolder look.

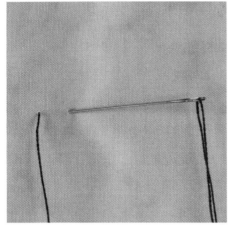 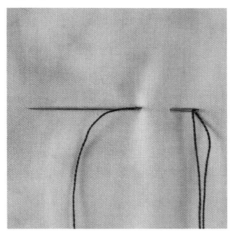 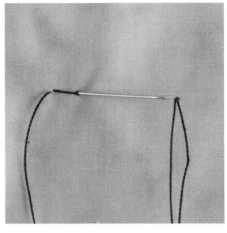

1 Review Starting the Stitch on page 124 to thread the needle and embed the knot in the batting along the line you will be stitching over. Make the first stitch going down through all three layers of the quilt.

2 Taking a backstitch, bring the needle back up where the stitch started.

3 Push the needle back down into the batting where the first stitch finished.

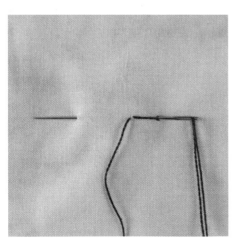 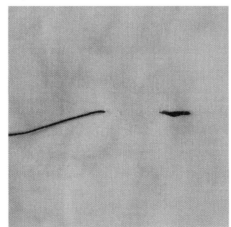 

4 Travel the needle through the batting. Bring it up the desired distance away, repeat steps 2 and 3 to begin the next stitch.

5 When there is approximately 6" of thread left in the needle, end your stitch and start a new length of thread. Refer to Ending the Stitch on page 125.

Crows Foot Stitch

The Crows Foot Stitch is similar to the embroidery Fly Stitch. It is most comfortably worked toward the quilter.

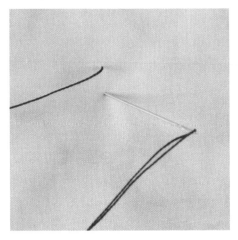

1 Review Starting the Stitch on page 124 to thread the needle and embed the knot in the batting along the line you will be stitching over. Working the stitches toward you, insert the needle down into all three layers of the quilt approximately 1/2" from the start of the stitch.

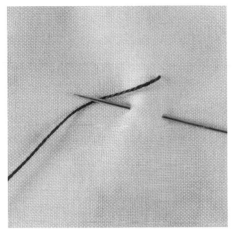

2 Bring the needle back up approximately 1/2" to the left of the first stitch.

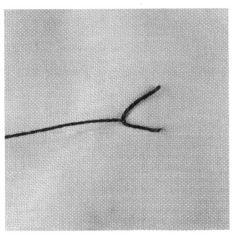

3 As you bring the needle up and pull the thread there will be a loop. Bring the needle up inside the loop and tighten the thread.

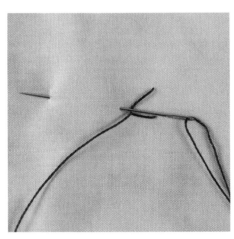

4 To keep the loop in place insert the needle into the top and batting, approximately 1/2" from the last stitch. Travel a needle's length from the first stitch and begin the next stitch.

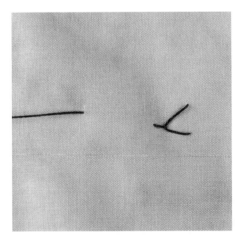

5 When there is approximately 6" of thread left in the needle, end your stitch and start a new length of thread. Refer to Ending the Stitch on page 125.

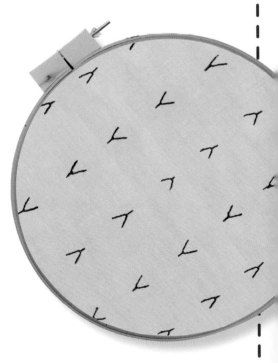

Buttonhole Stitch

The Buttonhole stitch is a slight variation of the Crow's Foot stitch. It is also easiest to achieve by stitching toward you.

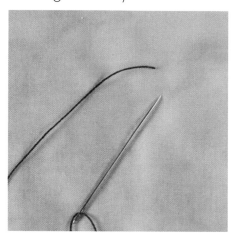

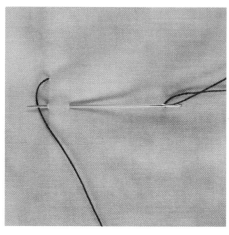

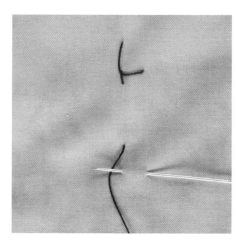

1 Review Starting the Stitch on page 124 to thread the needle and embed the knot in the batting along the line you will be stitching over.

2 Working the stitches toward you, insert the needle down into all three layers of the quilt approximately 1/2" below and slightly to the right of the start of the stitch. **Note:** If you are left-handed, your stitch will be slightly to the left of the start of the stitch.

Bring the needle back up, below where the thread first came out of the quilt. As you pull the thread there will be a loop. Make sure the needle is inside the loop. Tighten the thread.

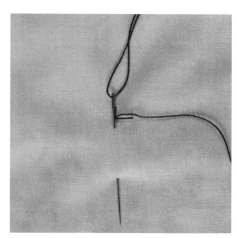

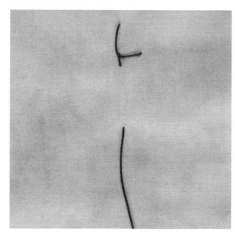

3 Insert the needle in the top and batting and make a small stitch to keep the loop in place.

4 Travel the needle through the batting the desired distance to begin the next stitch. Repeat to continue quilting.

5 When there is approximately 6" of thread left in the needle, end your stitch and start a new length thread. Refer to Ending the Stitch on page 125.

Running Cross Stitch

The Running Cross Stitch is similar to the Japanese Sashiko stitch called Ten (juujizashi). In this stitch rows of running stitches intersect to make little crosses. The stitches here are worked one at a time.

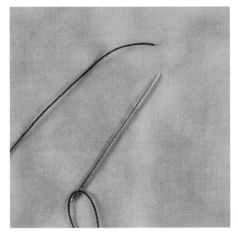

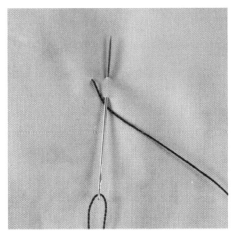

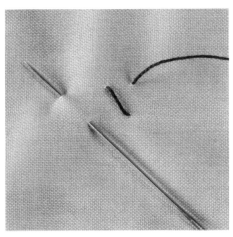

1 Review Starting the Stitch on page 124 to thread the needle and embed the knot in the batting along the line you will be stitching over.

2 Insert the needle through all three layers of the quilt forming a diagonal stitch.

3 Bring the needle back up at the top and to the right of the beginning stitch.

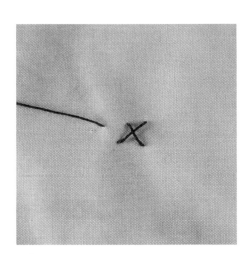

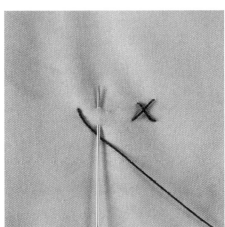

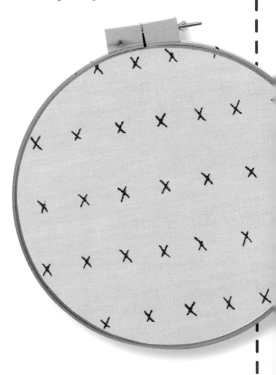

4 Insert the needle down into the top and batting, forming an "x" with the thread.

5 Travel the needle to the start of the next stitch. When there is approximately 6" of thread left in the needle, end your stitch and start a new length of thread. Refer to Ending the Stitch on page 125.

Marking Your Quilt Design

Making a Fan Design Template

To create the fan design on your quilt top, a template can be used. You can make your own template in any size by using a compass or round household item.

Using a Compass

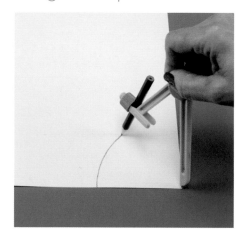

1 Set the compass to the arc size you desire. Place the compass in the corner of a sheet of paper and draw a quarter circle.

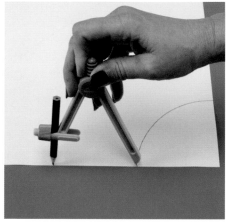

2 Move the compass to the point where the beginning quarter circle line touched the edge of the paper.

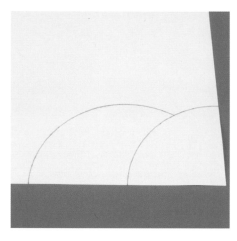

3 Draw another arc until it reaches the first arc.

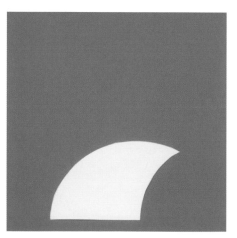

4 Cut out the second arc.

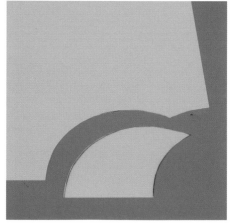

5 Trace your template design onto template plastic and cut out. See page 15 to trace onto your quilt.

Using a Round Object

1 Using a pencil and piece of paper, trace around a plate or other round object.

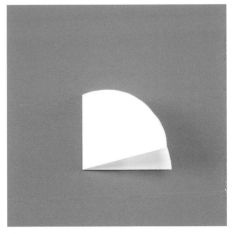

2 Cut out the traced circle and fold it into quarters.

3 Use this quarter to draw the first arc onto template plastic.

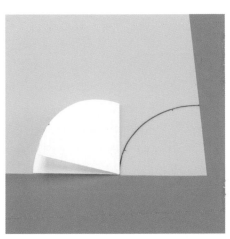

4 Keeping the paper folded, line up the straight folded edge with the curve of the first drawn arc.

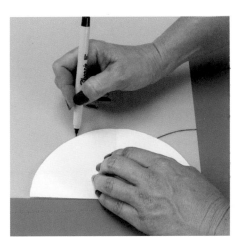

5 Unfold the quarter to make a half circle and draw around this shape until the line of the second arc meets the line of the first. Remove the paper circle.

6 Cut out the second drawn shape. This is the template for your fan quilting.

Marking the Fan Design

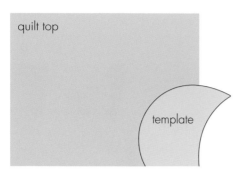

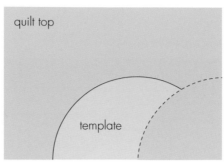

1 Place the fan template in the bottom right hand corner of the quilt, matching the straight edges. Draw around the arc of the template.

Note: Begin in the left hand corner if you are left handed.

2 Place the inner curve of the template against the outer curve of the first marked arc. Draw around the outer template curve.

3 Continue marking the bottom row of designs in this manner. When you come to the edge of the quilt, the design will run off the edge.

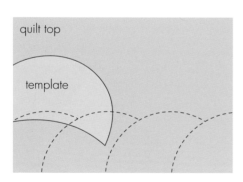

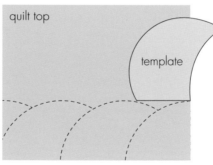

4 Position the template to turn the corner to begin the next row.

5 If you prefer, you may move the template and mark the next row directly above the first.

When you quilt the fan design, the marked outer arc will be quilted top to bottom. The unmarked inner arcs will be quilted the distance of the needle length or the width of your thumb knuckle. If you prefer you may mark the inner curves with dashed lines before quilting.

Note: The large marked arcs can contain varying numbers of smaller arcs. This is up to the individual quilter.

Amish Wave/Mennonite Fan Design

The fan design was so easy to execute that many individuals and church groups used it in their work. Therefore it became known by as many different names as the people who used it. Some of these design names include Amish Wave, Mennonite Fan, Baptist Fan and Wave.

The fan design is popular because...

- It is quilted on the bias which makes it easier to quilt
- The design covers the entire quilt, ignoring the piecing and acting as a unifying feature
- It can be stitched by any level of quilter
- It can be quilted by groups around a frame working from the outside edge toward the quilt center
- The fan design is often seen with single lines of quilting, but can also be worked with two or three lines of quilting

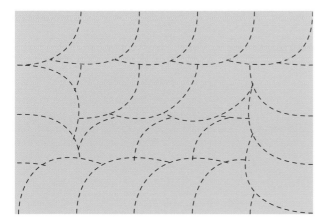

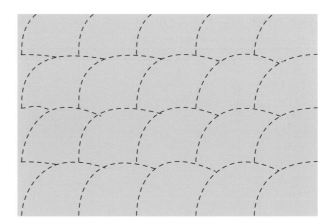

Fan shaped designs, such as the Amish Wave or Mennonite Fan, are quilted from the outside edge of the quilt and worked in toward the center. It can also be stitched in rows from bottom to top.

If you are quilting the fan design on a frame with rollers, you will quilt the design in rows.

Start at the bottom of the quilt and work toward the top, rolling the quilt as you go.

Thumb or Egg Cup Quilting

Thumb or egg cup quilting is worked from the smallest curve out toward the largest. All the fans should have the same number of curves, but may be slightly different sizes depending on the accuracy of the quilter.

Marking the Thumb/Egg Cup Design

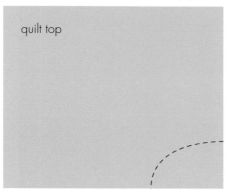

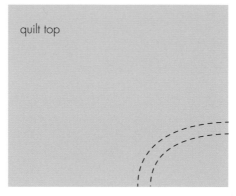

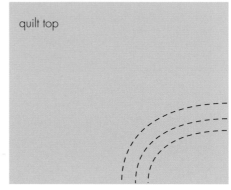

1   Begin by using your thumb to determine the size of the first curve. Mark around the curve.

Note: You may also use a small, circular household object such as an egg cup.

2   Mark the larger curves using the length of your needle or the width of your thumb to determine distance between lines. These arcs can be drawn freehand.

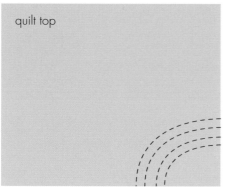

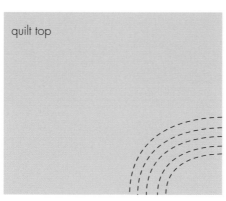

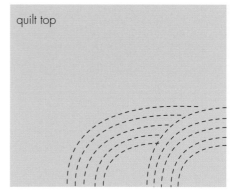

3   Stop marking when the fan design is the desired size. Begin marking the next fan, remembering to draw the same number of curves as the first fan. The subsequent sizes of your curves may vary slightly from those of the first fan.

When you quilt, the marked inner arc of the fan design will be quilted first. Work your way out toward the larger arcs.

Diagonal Lines or Cross Hatch Designs

The Navy quilt was simply quilted with one set of diagonal lines.

Lines and grids are easy to mark with a large rotary cutting ruler and a Hera, or you could use masking tape.

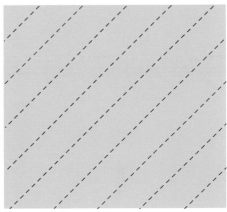

Decide which angle to use on the ruler and balance this up with the outside edge of the quilt. I used 60 degrees for this quilt, but 45 is popular.

If you want to then mark a second set of lines from the other side of the quilt, then you will be able to form a grid or cross hatch/diamond design.

As you quilt you can remove the basting stitches or pins as you work. When all the quilting is complete you prepare to bind the quilt. (See page 138.)

Hand Stitched Continuous Binding

A quilt can be finished from beginning to end, stitching by hand. This step-by-step for binding works for either hand or machine stitching.

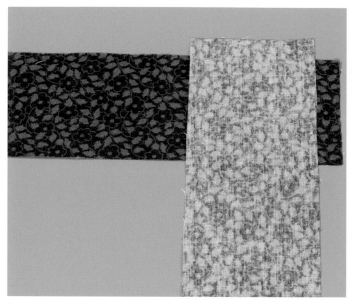

1 Cut strips of fabric for the binding 2-1/2" wide. Lay one of the strips right side up on a flat surface. Place a second strip wrong side up on the first, as shown.

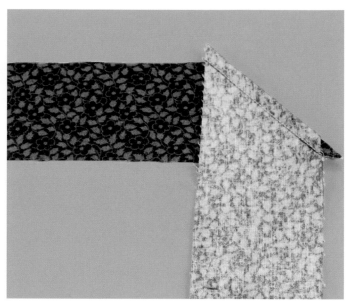

2 Draw a diagonal line from corner to corner beginning at the corner where the strips meet. Sew on the marked line and trim 1/4" from the sewn line.

3 Press the seams open. Continue to sew strips together in this way to make one continuous binding strip.

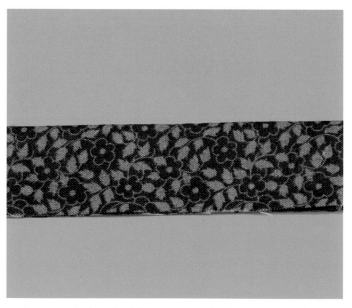

4 Press the length of the continuous binding strip in half, wrong sides together.

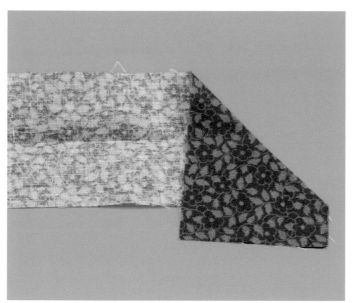

5 Unfold the binding strip and fold one end at a 45-degree angle. Press.

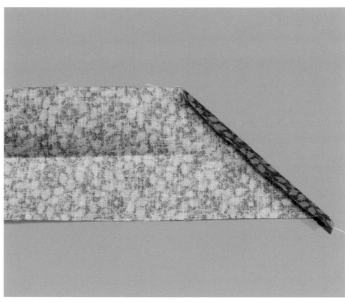

6 Trim 1/4" from the pressed fold.

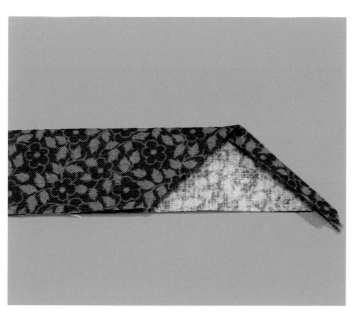

7 Refold and press the binding strip.

8 Trim the backing and batting even with the quilt top. Make sure all the layers are square and even.

9 Use a continuous backstitch to attach the binding to the quilt. The stitches need to go through all three layers to secure the binding. Align the raw angled edge of the binding strip with the raw edge of the quilt front at the center of one of the sides and pin. Begin stitching with a backstitch about 1/4" away from the angled edge of the binding strip. (**Note:** If you are machine stitching, use a walking foot and continue to align edges.)

10 Stitch through all three layers, removing pins as you go. Take a back stitch every inch or so to lock the seam stitches. Stop stitching about 1/4" away from the first corner. Secure with a few backstitches and leave your needle ready to turn the corner. (**Note:** If you are using your machine, backstitch and remove the quilt top from under the walking foot.)

11 Fold the binding strip to form a 45-degree mitered corner.

12 Bring the binding strip over to align with the raw edge of the quilt top.

Hand Stitched Continuous Binding Cont.

13   With your needle, take a few backstitches from the edge of the quilt and binding to secure the fold. Pin the binding to raw edge and continue stitching, repeating the process at each corner. (**Note:** For machine stitching, place quilt back under walking foot, repeating the process at each corner.)

14   Stop stitching when you are approximately 6" away from the beginning angled end of the binding strip. Trim the binding as needed to tuck into the angled end. Continue stitching to the beginning stitches. Backstitch to secure.

15   Turn the quilt over and fold the binding to the back, covering raw edges and overlapping the stitching on the back of the quilt. Pin in place, mitering binding at the corners.

16   Hand stitch the binding to the quilt, taking a backstitch every inch or so to lock seam stitches. At each corner, stitch down the miter, turn the quilt and continue stitching until all sides are sewn down.

color inspiration

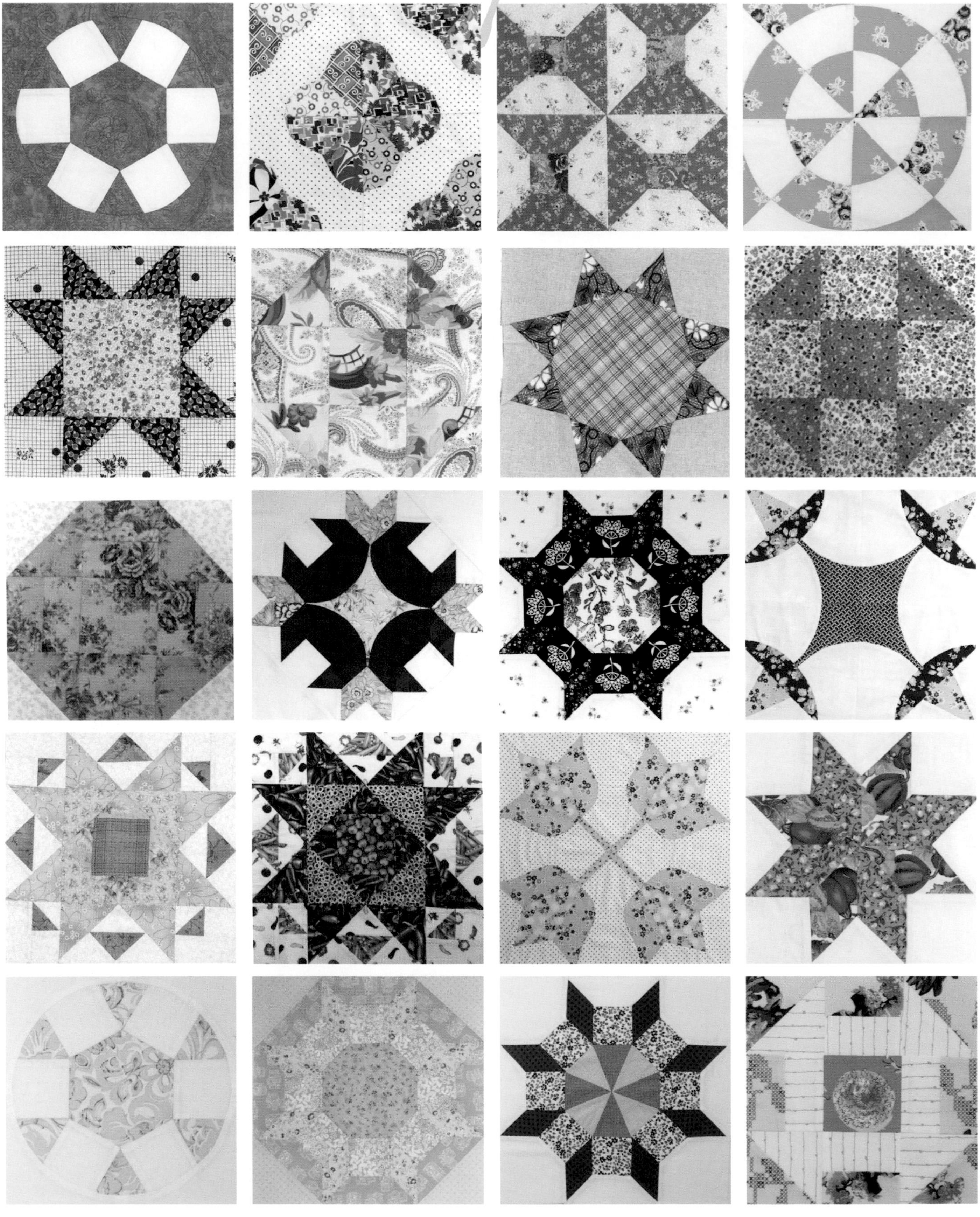

Other Landauer Books by Carolyn Forster

Hexagon Happenings
Landauer Publishing 2014
ISBN: 978-1-935726-66-1

Quilting-on-the-Go
Taking it Further
Landauer Publishing 2014
ISBN: 978-1-935726-50-0

Utility Quilting
Landauer Publishing 2011
ISBN: 978-1-935726-14-2

Supply Sources

Support and shop at your local quilt shop for supplies used in this book.

Quilting Hoops
https://www.cottonpatch.co.uk/acatalog/Quilting_Hoops.html

Needles
John James
https://www.jjneedles.com

Tulip
http://www.tulip-japan.co.jp/kyoutsu(englis)/syugei/koukyuhari.html

Wadding
Hobbs Heirloom (80/20)
Hobbs Organic with scrim

Template Plastic
https://quiltroom.co.uk

Hera Marker and Thimbles
http://www.clover-usa.com/en/

Cotton Perle
https://www.valdani.com/products/

Marking Pencils
http://www.sewline.com.au/product-range/

1/4" Wonder Wheel
https://www.amitie.com.au
http://www.seweasy.com

Utility Clips
https://www.amitie.com.au

Jinny Beyer Perfect Piecer
https://www.jinnybeyer.com

Quilters Quarter
http://www.prym.com/prym/proc/docs/index_en.html

Aurifil threads
http://www.aurifil.com

Matilda's Own Design Mat
http://www.victoriantextiles.com.au

Roc-Lon Multi Purpose Cloth
http://www.roc-lon.com/products/multi_purpose.html

Scissors
http://www.havelssewing.com

accuquilt
http://www.accuquilt.com